A TIME TO RETURN

THE RADICAL ACT THAT REVOLUTIONIZED MY RELATIONSHIP WITH MONEY

MARK GREAVES

Published by Freiling Agency, LLC.

P.O. Box 1264
Warrenton, VA 20188

www.FreilingAgency.com

PB ISBN: 978-1-963701-82-1
HB ISBN: 978-1-963701-83-8
E-book ISBN: 978-1-963701-84-5

CONTENTS

Introduction: The Word That Changed Everything........ v

PART 1

1 The Test We're Failing—And the Invitation
to Pass...3
2 Testing Is Normal—And Essential......................11
3 The Ten Plagues—A Test of Pride 19
4 The Ten Commandments—A Test of
Obedience..27
5 Malachi 3:10—The Only Time God Says
"Test Me" 37
6 The Ten Spies—A Test of Faith 53
7 The Ten Lepers—A Test of Gratitude.................69
8 The Ten Virgins—A Test of Readiness.................77

PART 2

9 From Emptiness to Purpose 85
10 Stories of Supernatural Provision.........................99
11 The Tithe Foundation—Kingdom Impact 111

PART 3

12 Starting Your Own Test......................................125
13 Beyond the Tithe—A Life of Generosity............139
14 The $161 Billion Vision 151
15 The Test That Never Ends..................................165

Conclusion: Pass the Test..177

"The tithe became the

key that unlocked a life of

purpose I never knew

was possible."

INTRODUCTION

THE WORD THAT CHANGED EVERYTHING

Tithing.

Honestly, I never thought I'd write a book about it.

For much of my life, I barely paid attention to the word. I knew tithing was a "church thing" that I was supposed to do, but I didn't do it—and truthfully, I didn't think it mattered much either way. When I was a kid, I thought tithing meant dropping money in the plate on Sunday. If my dad gave me a ten or a twenty to place in the offering basket, I thought it was cool. It felt instinctively good to be generous. I didn't know if it went toward helping the church keep the lights on or fund a mission trip. Never thought about it. At the time, I saw no difference between tithing and random giving.

Fast-forward to my adult years: Had I matured in my understanding? Not really. I wasn't tithing and had not yet looked into how God wanted to move in my life. I wasn't following God's Word closely. And even when

I did give, it was irregular, guilt-driven, and emotionally disconnected. Giving had become transactional, not transformational. But over time, God patiently revealed truths that changed everything for me. Truths that I pray will become real for you, too.

God doesn't hide His love in riddles. He is not vague or elusive. He reveals Himself clearly through His Word, through His people, and through everyday provision. He is always faithful, always pursuing. But there's a catch: He wants our hearts, not our leftovers. He wants to be first—not because He needs anything from us, but because He knows what happens when He is.

I can tell you firsthand how the word tithe has changed my life.

Before tithing, I was not only keeping 100% of my earnings for my purposes, but I was also thinking mostly about my personal journey and the things that I wanted. Now I know why God described the thoughts of men at the time of Noah as "Only evil, all the time." The problem with living inside my subjective point of view was that what I wanted was constantly changing. The world around me was shifting. New targets would emerge not just annually, but monthly. New cars and body styles roll out each year. New homes are intriguing when they're in areas that you'd rather spend time in. New vacations always seem to be the answer to unwind. New work goals seem to rise and fall with an ever-changing market and a constant need to compete. Most of my goals revolved around growth for the sake of it, especially at work.

It's a peculiar kind of prison when you have everything you thought you wanted but find yourself more restless than ever. Success, as I had defined it, became a treadmill that only moved faster the longer I stayed on it. Each achievement felt hollow within weeks of reaching it. Each promotion brought new pressures that the last promotion was supposed to eliminate. I found myself asking dangerous questions in the quiet moments: Is this all there is? Have I wasted my life chasing shadows?

The truth is, I was living what many would call the American Dream, but I was suffocating inside it. I had confused motion with progress, accumulation with abundance. I was building a kingdom, but it was a kingdom of one, and kingdoms of one are inherently unstable. They collapse under their own weight because there's no foundation strong enough to support a life built entirely on self.

As President of a large financial institution, growth was something I was used to aiming at. If you're not growing, you're dying... and I still agree with that. The issue with certain types of growth is not tactics or pursuits, but our reasons and purpose. Eventually, everyone wants to know why they do what they do, who it impacts beyond just numbers, and what they'll be remembered for if they complete it well. In my case, I continued to ask these questions with no certain answers.

I did my job because that's what was called for. I worked hard because that's who I was. I told myself that I did it because I really cared about the customer. I told myself that my legacy would be building something "special". Really, I just lied to myself to keep it all going. In reality, what I sold was the same thing that hundreds of other companies had access to. Sure, I wanted to do a good job for the clients of our company, but no one really talked much about the customer during our internal meetings. It was all about us, all the time. My legacy would have become building something for my own personal benefit, and selling myself that I was doing it for others. I was full of crap, and I knew it.

The weight of this realization was crushing. I had spent years climbing what I thought was the mountain, only to discover I had been digging a hole. The higher I climbed in my career, the deeper I seemed to sink into meaninglessness. I was successful by every metric that mattered to the world, but spiritually bankrupt by the only metric that mattered to eternity. The disconnect between my public success and private emptiness created a kind of spiritual whiplash that left me questioning everything I thought I knew about life, purpose, and what it meant to truly prosper.

This internal reckoning wasn't just about work—it was about identity. Who was I when the titles were stripped away? What did I have to offer the world beyond my ability to generate revenue? These questions haunted me because I couldn't answer them with any confidence. I had become so accustomed to measuring my worth by my output that I had forgotten I was created for relationship, not just productivity.

This led to a deep internal struggle. I wanted more out of life. I knew I had to work. Didn't have a choice. But I no longer felt connected to my work. I felt like I was short-changing my family, so I could continue with a façade that I'd created, and didn't want it all to fall apart. At times, I wished my life would just be over. I was exhausted, afraid, and empty. This is what a life of knocking down goal after goal, paycheck after paycheck, and reward after reward had earned me. Emptiness, brokenness, and a desire for it all to end rather than being excited for where it might lead. I coped with the stress poorly. I drank. I did my best to numb the feelings of emptiness the best that I could. Then, God showed me another way.

I heard my first message on tithing late in 2020. Our Pastor took us on a journey one Sunday that totally unlocked what had been missing for me before. It's like my spiritual eyes were finally opened. Thank God. My work could mean so much more, but it wouldn't unless I understood the provider and master whom I served.

God wasn't just after my money. He was after my heart. Not because he wanted to keep score, but because he wants to bless me. The tithe is an invitation to so much more. A life of endless meaning. A way for me to attach my temporary effort to eternal significance. It became a gateway for me to understand and know the eternal creator of the universe in a personal and unique way. By tithing, I was able to see the fruit of my labor play out in the lives of others and live under a blessing that I never thought possible.

What struck me most about that message wasn't the mechanics of giving ten percent—it was the revelation that God wanted to partner with me in something bigger than my own ambitions. For the first time in years, I felt a sense of alignment that transcended my circumstances. The tithe wasn't just about money leaving my account; it was about invitation entering my heart. An invitation to participate in God's work in the world, to see my resources as tools for His kingdom rather than monuments to my own success.

This shift in perspective didn't happen overnight, but when it did happen, it was seismic. Suddenly, my work had eternal weight to it. My income became a stewardship rather than just a scoreboard. My daily decisions carried the potential to impact lives beyond my own family tree. The tithe became the key that unlocked a life of purpose I never knew was possible.

It's why I now do what I do. The same thing I did before, under a new logo. Tithe Lending was born from the bottom of a personal pit that I was in while seemingly on top of the mountain. Honoring God has become our mission. Loving our neighbor, our tactics. Putting God first through the tithe is a discipline that has transformed our hearts and our work. I have several stories to tell about the faithfulness of God to us throughout this journey. I want these same blessings for you. God wants to transform you from the inside, and he gives us a very specific way that can assist him throughout Scripture. The tithe changed my life, and I believe it's a time to return to this principle in America and allow it to change yours as well.

Not too long ago, I found myself in a church that preached directly from Scripture, verse by verse, truth by truth. When I encountered the reality that tithing is not about money, but about the heart, I was ashamed of how casually I had dismissed it. But more than that, I was awakened. What began as a reluctant learning curve became a joyful calling. I began to see how God uses the tithe to restore our priorities, reset our hearts, and build His kingdom through His people.

This book is not a theory. It's testimony.

I spent decades building a career in the mortgage industry, eventually becoming the President of a large outfit employing over 3,000 people. In 2022, I stepped away from that role to found Tithe Lending, a mortgage business committed to giving 10% of revenue—not profit—to gospel-centered causes through the Tithe Foundation. In 2024, our tithe represented over 62% of company profits. We were humbled and thrilled to return those funds to the Lord to support the local church, Christian education, youth and family services, and ministries serving the homeless.

For me, this is not just about business. It's about building a legacy that honors God first, attracts more people to His son Jesus, and invests in the lives of others in need. It's about seeing every dollar as a tool for worship and every act of obedience as a doorway to joy. The tithe has changed the way I live, lead, and love. It has made God #1 in my heart, and through that alignment, He has worked in ways I could never have orchestrated on my own.

I want that for you. I believe it's what God wants for you.

So let's journey together.

PART 1

"From the very beginning, God embedded the principle of giving first into the rhythm of His people."

1

THE TEST WE'RE FAILING— AND THE INVITATION TO PASS

Tithing is a test.

Most of us have heard that before, but very few of us understand what that really means. In fact, if "tithe" were on a vocabulary test, the average American—Christian or not—would probably get it wrong.

Let's start simply: The word tithe means "tenth." In Hebrew, one word used is *maaser*, a masculine noun meaning a tenth part. But in Scripture, it's not just any tenth. It's the first tenth. This is key. Tithing is about priority, not just percentage.

From the very beginning, God embedded the principle of giving first into the rhythm of His people. Cain and Abel's story in Genesis 4 is one of the first places we see this. Cain brought some of his fruits, but Abel brought the firstborn of his flock. One gave leftovers. The other gave first. And God responded accordingly.

Not because He needed a sheep, but because He saw Abel's heart.

Think about what this tells us about the nature of God. He doesn't need our money—He owns the cattle on a thousand hills. He doesn't need our resources—He spoke the universe into existence. What he desires is our trust. Our willingness to put Him first, even when it feels risky or uncomfortable. The tithe is less about the transaction and more about the transformation that happens when we choose to honor God with our first and best.

This principle echoes throughout Scripture. Abraham gave a tenth to Melchizedek after his victory in battle, not because he was commanded to, but because something in his heart recognized that his success came from a source beyond himself. Jacob promised to give God a tenth of everything he received, making it a cornerstone of his covenant relationship with the Almighty. These weren't reluctant religious obligations; they were expressions of worship and acknowledgment of God's provision.

Here's the hard truth: Today, as a nation, we are largely failing the test of tithing. But with that failure comes incredible opportunity.

Barna Research tells us that only 39% of U.S. adults can correctly define "tithing." Among Christians, that number rises just slightly to 43%. And unsurprisingly, our practice reflects our ignorance. Only 4% of American households tithe to their local church. Include other nonprofits, and it rises to just 6%. The average annual giving? Just $895 per household.

These statistics reveal something deeper than financial habits—they expose a crisis of discipleship. We've somehow convinced ourselves that following Jesus is about everything except our wallets. We'll sing loudly on Sunday, attend Bible study on Wednesday, and serve in the nursery on rotation, but when it comes to our finances, we operate as if God has no claim on our resources. This compartmentalization of faith is foreign to biblical Christianity, where every aspect of life—including our money—is under the lordship of Christ.

The tragedy is that we're not just failing a test; we're missing an invitation to experience God's faithfulness in ways that would absolutely transform our lives. Every unpaid tithe represents a missed opportunity to see God work miracles in our finances, our families, and our communities. We're choosing to live as spiritual paupers when God has invited us to be kingdom partners.

Yes, we live in uncertain economic times. Yes, inflation is real. But this isn't just about economics—it's about our priorities. During the Great Depression, when food and money were far scarcer, Christians gave an average of 3.3% of their income to the church. In 2024, we're down to 2.5%. Despite living in the wealthiest nation on earth, our hearts—and our hands—are more closed than ever.

This decline isn't happening in a vacuum. It's happening in the context of unprecedented prosperity. The average American household has more disposable income, more conveniences, and more luxuries than royalty enjoyed just centuries ago. Yet our giving has decreased. We have more, but we give less. We're more blessed, but less grateful. We're more prosperous, but less generous.

What does this say about our relationship with money? What does it reveal about our trust in God? When we have abundance but hold it tightly, we're essentially declaring that our security comes from our bank account rather than our Savior. We're worshipping the gift instead of the Giver.

The irony is palpable: We live in a culture obsessed with financial advice, investment strategies, and wealth building, yet we ignore the one financial principle that comes with a divine guarantee. God literally challenges us to test Him in this area—to see if He won't "throw open the floodgates of heaven and pour out so much blessing that there will not be room enough to store it" (Malachi 3:10). No financial advisor can offer that kind of return on investment.

Now here's the hopeful part:

If just American Christians tithed 10%, we would release $161 billion in new resources annually. Let that sink in. $161 billion for orphan care, clean water,

Bible translation, addiction recovery, church planting, Christian education, local missions, and global evangelism. Imagine what would happen if we simply obeyed what God has always asked of us.

For illustration purposes, let me break down what $161 billion annually would do in our current world. Let's imagine that each issue was addressed one year at a time. In just a decade, look at what would be accomplished on earth by returning the tithe to our Lord. In doing so, He would assist us in making Earth look much more like heaven.

Christian Schools: With $12 million per school (including construction and first-year operating costs), we could open 13,416 schools annually. That's right— over 13,000 schools could be built, opened, and funded each year.

Homeless Meals: At $2.50 per meal, including logistics, we could serve 64.4 billion meals per year. World hunger would be largely eradicated.

Youth Centers: At $3.25 million per center, including construction and setup, we could open 49,538 teen and youth centers annually. Giving our kids safe places to go after school would no longer be an issue.

Mission Trips: At $3,000 per person, we could fund 53.67 million international mission trips yearly. Imagine the spreading of the Gospel and assistance provided to those in the most need.

Education Grants: With $10,000 per student, we could provide 16.1 million scholarships annually. What would that do to transform our world if 16 million students received grants to Christian universities?

Clean Water Wells: At $10,000 per well serving 500-1,000 people, we could build 16.1 million wells yearly. Clean water access could be solved globally within one year of faithful tithing.

Bible Translations: Including translation and printing costs, we could fund Bible translations for 292,727 new languages annually. The entire world would have God's printed word in their own language.

Homeless Veterans: At $25,000 per veteran for permanent supportive housing, we could house 6.44 million veterans yearly. Our veteran population would be completely cared for.

Child Trafficking Rescue: At $10,000 per child for rescue, rehabilitation, and reintegration, we could help 16.1 million children annually escape trafficking.

This level of funding could revolutionize global impact for the Church. From massive educational and evangelistic efforts to tangible acts of compassion, $161 billion isn't just a number—it represents the power to serve billions and transform generations in Jesus' name.

But here's what moves me most about these numbers: They represent more than organizational impact—they represent individual transformation. Every person who chooses to tithe doesn't just contribute to these larger outcomes; they personally experience the joy of partnership with God. They discover that obedience leads to abundance, that generosity generates blessing, and that putting God first doesn't diminish their lives—it multiplies them.

The tithe isn't a tax—it's an invitation. A test that leads to abundance.

"God is not looking for your wallet. He's looking for your worship."

2

TESTING IS NORMAL— AND ESSENTIAL

If we're going to take tithing seriously as a test, we need to understand something deeper about how God works: **He tests what He loves.**

That might sound backward. We tend to associate testing with punishment or pressure. But in Scripture, testing is a way God **refines, prepares, and blesses** His people. His tests are never pointless. They always reveal something, and they always *invite* us closer to Him.

In fact, many of the most well-known moments in the Bible involve tests that required trust, obedience, and often great personal cost. And often, the number **10** is connected to these tests.

Consider Abraham's test on Mount Moriah. God asked him to sacrifice Isaac, not because God delighted in potential tragedy, but because He wanted to reveal the depth of Abraham's faith. The test wasn't about what Abraham would lose; it was about what Abraham would discover about God's faithfulness. When Abraham raised the knife, he found a ram in the thicket. When he was willing to give up everything, he received everything back multiplied. This is the pattern of divine testing: apparent loss leading to abundant gain.

Or think about Job's trials. Satan convinced God to test Job's faithfulness by allowing tremendous suffering. Job lost his wealth, his health, his family—everything except his life and his faith. Yet through the test, Job discovered truths about God's character that prosperity could never have taught him. "Though he slay me, yet will I hope in him," Job declared. The test revealed that Job's relationship with God was deeper than his circumstances. And in the end, God restored everything Job had lost, doubled.

The Israelites faced test after test in the wilderness. Ten plagues in Egypt. Ten times they grumbled against Moses. The golden calf incident. The report of the twelve spies. Each test was an opportunity to choose trust over fear, obedience over rebellion, faith over sight. Some tests they passed; others they failed spectacularly. But each one revealed the condition of their hearts and their readiness—or lack thereof—to enter the Promised Land.

Even Jesus faced testing. Forty days in the wilderness. Three temptations. Each one was designed to reveal whether Jesus would choose the Father's will over immediate gratification, earthly power, or spectacular display.

The test wasn't about Satan's power; it was about Jesus' identity and mission. And when Jesus passed the test, angels came to minister to Him.

The pattern is clear: God's tests are never arbitrary. They're always purposeful. They reveal character, develop faith, and prepare us for greater blessing and responsibility.

Let me walk you through several tests from Scripture that apply to us today... and they're ever present in the decision to tithe.

These stories aren't just ancient history. They are pictures of our daily walk with God. And every one of them carries the same pattern:

- God calls.
- People respond—or resist.
- The heart is revealed.
- Blessing or consequence follows.

This pattern plays out in every significant biblical narrative. Noah faced the test of building an ark when there was no sign of rain. His neighbors mocked him, but his obedience saved humanity. Daniel faced the test of dietary laws in a foreign land, then later the test of prayer when it was outlawed. His faithfulness established him as one of history's greatest examples of integrity under pressure.

The three Hebrew boys—Shadrach, Meshach, and Abednego—faced the ultimate test of loyalty when commanded to bow to Nebuchadnezzar's golden image. Their response reveals the heart of someone who has passed God's tests: "If we are thrown into the blazing furnace, the God we serve is able to deliver us from it, and he will deliver us from Your Majesty's hand. But even if he does not, we want you to know, Your Majesty, that we will not serve your gods or worship the image of gold you have set up." This is faith that has been tested and proven.

What's remarkable about these tests is how they often involve the number ten or principles of giving the first and best. Ten plagues. Ten Commandments. Ten virgins. Ten talents. Ten lepers. The tithe—the tenth. God seems to use this number to signify completeness, wholeness, and the fullness of our surrender to Him.

So let me be honest: **Tithing is a test.**

But it's not a test to shame you. It's a test to **form you**.

God is not looking for your wallet—He's looking for your worship. He's after your heart. And he knows that what we do with our *first tenth* reveals what's most important to us.

This is why the tithe is so revealing. It's not just about the money—it's about the heart behind the money.

When we tithe, we're declaring that God is more trust-worthy than our savings account. We're saying that His kingdom is more important than our comfort. We're choosing eternal investment over temporal security.

The test of tithing exposes our deepest beliefs about God's character. Do we really believe He's a good Father who takes care of His children? Do we trust that He sees our needs and will provide? Do we have confidence that His ways are higher than our ways? The tithe answers these questions more honestly than any theological statement we might make.

We struggle with the tithe because we see it as a loss. We measure it in *dollars*, not in *devotion*. When our income rises, 10% feels harder to release. We think of vacations, bills, savings, and dreams. Earthly things.

This perspective reveals how easily we can fall into the trap of measuring God's blessings by our earthly accumulations rather than by our spiritual growth. We calculate what we could do with that 10%—the extra house payment, the vacation fund, the emergency savings—and we convince ourselves that keeping it is the "responsible" thing to do. But what we're really doing is choosing to trust in our own planning over God's provision.

The irony is that the more God blesses us finan-cially, the harder it becomes to tithe. When you're making $30,000 a year, tithing $3,000 feels significant but manageable. When you're making $300,000 a year, tithing $30,000 feels enormous. The percentage hasn't changed, but our attachment to the amount has grown. This is precisely why tithing is such an effective test—it reveals whether our trust in God grows with our income or shrinks with our increasing sense of financial security.

But to God, the tithe is not about giving something *up*—it's about lifting something *up*. It's not a subtraction from our wealth, but an alignment of our hearts. It says, "God, You're first." It declares, "I trust you more than my bank account."

When we understand tithing as alignment rather than loss, everything changes. We stop seeing it as God taking from us and start seeing it as God inviting us into partnership with Him. We stop viewing it as a financial burden and start experiencing it as a spiritual privilege. We stop calculating what we're giving up and start anticipating what God wants to give us.

This shift in perspective transforms the entire experience of tithing. Instead of reluctantly writing a check, we joyfully invest in God's kingdom. Instead of feeling depleted, we feel connected to something bigger than ourselves. Instead of worrying about what we won't have, we get excited about what God might do.

Colossians 3:2 says, "Set your minds on things above, not on earthly things." Tithing does exactly that. It lifts our gaze. It unlocks our grip. It opens our hearts.

And in that simple act of obedience, we pass the test—not by acing it, but by **trusting** the One who gives the test in the first place.

"My pride, disguised as wisdom, was actually limiting my ability to be the generous person I claimed to want to be."

3

THE TEN PLAGUES—A TEST OF PRIDE

In the book of *Exodus*, God sends ten devastating plagues upon Egypt—not because He needed ten tries to free the Israelites, but because He was testing Pharaoh's heart. Each plague directly challenged the authority of Egypt's false gods, exposing them as powerless in the face of the one true God. This wasn't just about freeing slaves—it was about confronting pride, rebellion, and misplaced worship. And each time Pharaoh was given a chance to humble himself, he refused. He clung to control, hardened his heart, and ultimately paid the price.

The progression of the plagues tells a story of escalating confrontation between divine authority and human pride. The first plague turned the Nile—Egypt's lifeline and a symbol of their god Hapi—into blood. The second brought frogs, mocking the goddess Heqet. The third brought gnats, challenging the priests' ability to perform their rituals in a state of ceremonial cleanliness. With each plague, God was systematically dismantling the Egyptian pantheon, proving that their gods were nothing more than carved stone and human imagination.

But here's what strikes me most about this account: after each plague, Pharaoh had moments of apparent repentance. He would call for Moses and Aaron, promise to let the people go, and even ask them to pray for him. But as soon as the pressure lifted, he would change his mind and harden his heart again. This wasn't just stubbornness—it was a pattern of spiritual pride that couldn't bear the thought of submitting to authority beyond itself.

Pharaoh's pride manifested in a very specific way: he kept trying to negotiate with God. He offered compromises—let the men go, but keep the women and children. Let everyone go, but leave the livestock. Go, but don't go too far. These weren't genuine attempts at obedience; they were attempts to maintain control while appearing to comply. Pharaoh wanted to give God just enough to make the problems go away, but not enough to actually surrender his authority.

The lesson is clear: when God tests us, He isn't trying to take something from us—He's trying to free us. Pharaoh's downfall was pride. He believed he could maintain power, resist God, and still hold on to everything he valued. But in the end, pride cost him everything.

I know that test all too well.

While my modern life looked different from ancient Egypt, the spirit of Pharaoh still lurked in my heart. Pharaohs saw themselves as divine guardians of order, masters of their own fate. I wouldn't have claimed to be a god, but I certainly took pride in my ability to control outcomes. Throughout my career, I prided myself on navigating complexity, solving problems, making smart decisions, and leading others through chaos. That ability opened doors and earned respect, but it also became a spiritual trap.

The corporate world rewards this kind of thinking. We're taught to trust our instincts, rely on our expertise, and take credit for our successes. Performance reviews don't include categories for "dependence on God" or "recognition of divine provision." Instead, they measure our ability to deliver results through our own capabilities. Over time, this environment shaped my identity. I began to see myself as the primary architect of my success, the one responsible for generating the outcomes that mattered.

This pride wasn't overt or obviously sinful. It was subtle, professional, and socially acceptable. I wasn't boasting or being arrogant in obvious ways. I was simply operating from the assumption that my intelligence, work ethic, and decision-making ability were the primary factors in my financial success. This assumption felt reasonable, even responsible. But it was actually a form of practical atheism—living as if God's role in my life was minimal and my role was maximum.

When it came to my finances—especially giving—I wanted to stay in control. After all, it was *my* money. I had earned it, managed it, and multiplied it. Why should I hand over ten percent to God on principle? I figured I could give on *my* terms, in *my* time, to *my* causes. Surely my wisdom in giving would be just as effective as God's command to tithe.

This reasoning felt sophisticated and strategic. I convinced myself that I could be more effective with my giving if I researched the causes, timed the donations for maximum tax benefit, and chose recipients based on my personal values and interests. The tithe seemed rigid and outdated compared to my thoughtful, customized approach to generosity.

But underneath this rational veneer was the same spirit that drove Pharaoh to negotiate with God. I was trying to maintain control over my resources while appearing to be generous. I wanted to give God enough to feel good about my spirituality, but not enough to actually surrender my financial autonomy. I was attempting to be both generous and sovereign—a contradiction that reveals the depth of pride in the human heart.

The irony is that my "strategic" approach to giving actually produced less generosity than simple obedience would have. When I controlled the timing, I delayed.

When I controlled the amount, I gave less. When I controlled the recipients, I chose based on my comfort level rather than God's direction. My pride, disguised as wisdom, was actually limiting my ability to be the generous person I claimed to want to be.

But I was wrong.

That mindset, though logical on the surface, was rooted in the same pride that plagued Pharaoh. It took me years to realize that my desire to stay in control was actually keeping me in bondage. My refusal to submit to God's instruction wasn't just disobedience—it was self-deception. I thought I was preserving my power, but I was actually forfeiting peace.

The bondage of financial pride is particularly insidious because it masquerades as responsibility. We tell ourselves we're being good stewards when we're actually being controlling. We convince ourselves we're being wise when we're actually being fearful. We believe we're being generous when we're actually being selective. This self-deception can persist for years because it's reinforced by a culture that celebrates financial independence and personal control.

But here's what I discovered: the anxiety that comes with financial control is exhausting. When you believe you're responsible for generating, protecting, and directing all your resources, the pressure is overwhelming. Every market fluctuation becomes a personal threat. Every unexpected expense becomes a crisis. Every financial decision carries the weight of your entire future. This isn't freedom—it's slavery disguised as autonomy.

I can now say from experience: there is *freedom* in surrender. Tithing isn't about loss—it's about trust. When I finally released my grip and honored God with the first ten percent of my income, I didn't feel depleted. I felt *liberated*. The anxiety, the pressure, the illusion of self-sufficiency—all of it began to fade.

The freedom came not just from the act of giving, but from the acknowledgment that God was the true source of my provision. When I tithed, I was declaring that my income didn't originate with my abilities but with His blessing. This shift in perspective transformed not just my giving, but my entire relationship with money. I began to see my resources as tools for worship rather than monuments to my success.

If you're standing at that crossroads—where your pride meets God's test—don't wait. Don't go the way of Pharaoh. Don't cling to what you can't keep and miss out on what only God can give. Pass the test. Choose freedom. Surrender to the One who's not trying to take from you, but trying to lead you into something far better.

"Selective obedience is one
of the most common forms
of spiritual pride."

4

THE TEN COMMANDMENTS—A TEST OF OBEDIENCE

When God delivered Israel from slavery in Egypt, He didn't just lead them into freedom—He led them into a *relationship*. And that relationship came with a covenant: **the 10 Commandments**. These weren't arbitrary rules or outdated religious traditions. There were clear, divine instructions about how to love God and how to love others.

They weren't meant to crush, but to *guide*. Not to burden, but to *bless*. And in giving them, **God was testing His people,** not just their behavior, but their hearts. Would they walk in holiness when no one was watching? Would they trust His way even when it felt restrictive? Time and time again, Israel failed this test. And yet, each time, God's discipline wasn't about rejection—it was about restoration.

The context of the Ten Commandments reveals something profound about God's heart. These weren't the words of a distant deity imposing restrictions on reluctant subjects. These were the words of a loving Father establishing the boundaries that would allow His children to flourish. God had just rescued Israel from 400 years of bondage—He wasn't about to lead them into a different kind of slavery. He was giving them the framework for freedom.

Consider the first commandment: "You shall have no other gods before me." This wasn't divine jealousy—it was divine protection. God knew that when we worship anything other than Him, we become enslaved to it. Money, power, pleasure, reputation—these make terrible masters. They demand everything and deliver nothing. The first commandment isn't about limiting our worship; it's about directing our worship toward the only One worthy of it.

The same principle applies to each commandment. "Remember the Sabbath day, to keep it holy" wasn't about restricting productivity—it was about protecting our humanity. God knew that people created in His image need rest, reflection, and relationship. The Sabbath was a gift, not a burden. "Honor your father and mother" wasn't about blind obedience to flawed parents—it was about recognizing the importance of family structure and generational wisdom in a healthy society.

But here's what Israel discovered, and what we discover: knowing God's commands and following them are two different things. The test wasn't whether they could memorize the commandments—it was whether they would live by them when it cost them something.

I've come to see this test not just in Israel's story, but in my own.

For a long time, I saw God's commands as legalistic. Overbearing. Maybe even outdated. In reality, I just didn't want to give up control. I wanted to live life *my* way—with just enough obedience to feel spiritual, but not enough to feel surrendered.

This selective obedience is one of the most common forms of spiritual pride. We convince ourselves that we're following God while actually following our own interpretation of what God wants. We pick and choose which commands feel reasonable, which ones align with our lifestyle, and which ones we can safely ignore without feeling too guilty.

The danger of this approach is that it makes us the ultimate authority over Scripture rather than submitting to Scripture as the ultimate authority over us. We become editors of God's word rather than students of it. We treat the Bible like a buffet rather than a blueprint. This isn't just disobedience—it's a fundamental misunderstanding of the relationship between Creator and creation.

Sure, I could avoid the "big ones"—murder, adultery, theft. But others? **Keeping the Sabbath?** *Who has time for that? ***Honoring my father and mother?** *Depends on the day. ***Not coveting?** *Well, isn't comparison part of business?*

This rationalization reveals how easily we can compartmentalize our faith. We treat some commandments as non-negotiable while treating others as suggestions. We'll never commit murder, but we'll murder someone's reputation with gossip. We won't steal money, but we'll steal time from our families for work. We won't commit adultery, but we'll commit spiritual adultery by putting our careers before our calling.

The Sabbath was particularly challenging for me because it directly conflicted with my identity as someone who could always push harder, work longer, and achieve more. Rest felt like weakness. Margin felt like a wasted opportunity. I had bought into the cultural lie that busyness equals importance and that constant productivity equals faithfulness.

But God's command to rest wasn't about laziness—it was about trust. When I rested, I was declaring that the world could function without my constant input. When I took a Sabbath, I was acknowledging that God was more capable of sustaining my business than my 24/7 effort. This kind of trust was terrifying because it required me to believe that God cared more about my success than I did.

The commandment about honoring parents was equally challenging, not because my parents were difficult, but because honoring them required humility. It meant acknowledging that I didn't have all the answers, that their wisdom and experience had value, and that my independence wasn't as complete as I wanted to believe. In a culture that celebrates self-made success, honoring parents can feel like admitting weakness.

And coveting? In the business world, coveting is often disguised as market research, competitive analysis, or strategic planning. We call it "staying aware of the competition," but often it's just old-fashioned envy dressed up in professional language. We look at other companies' success, other leaders' achievements, and other people's lifestyles, and we want what they have. This desire drives us to work harder, but it also drives us away from contentment and gratitude.

What I now realize is that I wasn't struggling with rules. I was struggling with a **hardened heart**.

My life was driven by desire, not for bad things, but for "more" things: more income, more properties, more influence, more opportunities. I thought I was building a life of freedom, but what I was really doing was building a prison of my own making. I wasn't just burning the candle at both ends—I'd thrown the whole candle in the microwave and hit 'start.'

This pursuit of "more" is perhaps the most socially acceptable form of idolatry in our culture. We don't bow down to golden calves, but we do bow down to golden opportunities. We don't worship carved images, but we do worship the image we're trying to create of ourselves. We don't serve foreign gods, but we do serve the god of advancement, achievement, and accumulation.

The tragedy is that this god promises everything and delivers nothing. Each achievement creates a new hunger for the next one. Each acquisition reveals how empty material possessions really are. Each level of success just exposes how much further we think we need to go. We're running on a treadmill that only speeds up the faster we run.

More houses meant more stress. More titles meant more pressure. More vacations just meant I was working somewhere else.

What I thought would fulfill me ended up draining me.

This is the cruel irony of a life driven by "more." The very things we think will give us freedom actually enslave us. More possessions mean more things to maintain, protect, and worry about. More responsibilities mean more pressure and less margin. More opportunities mean more decisions and less peace.

I was living proof that you can gain the whole world and lose your soul. I had achieved what many people dream of, but I was empty inside. I had everything I thought I wanted, but I was miserable. I had reached the top of the mountain, only to discover it was the wrong mountain entirely.

And in the middle of all that striving, I kept pushing God's commands to the side—especially the ones that asked for margin, for trust, for rest, for submission. But God, in His mercy, didn't stop testing me. He kept inviting me back.

That's why the tithe is so powerful. It's not just about money—it's a **test of obedience**. Like the commandments, it's not a box to check, but a boundary that protects. It reminds us: *God is first.* His way is better. And obedience isn't about rule-following—it's about heart-alignment.

The tithe cuts through all our spiritual rationalization and gets to the heart of the matter: Do we trust God enough to obey Him when it costs us something? Will we follow His commands even when they don't make sense to our natural minds? Are we willing to put His kingdom before our comfort?

These questions reveal the true test of obedience. It's not about perfect performance—it's about humble submission. It's not about never struggling with God's commands—it's about choosing to follow them even when we struggle.

The truth is, I failed this test for a while. But I thank God daily that He doesn't give up on us. When I finally began to embrace His word—not just the parts I liked—His peace followed. His provision became clearer. And my life, while not easier, became more aligned and more fruitful.

God's word *always* works. And like Israel, we'll either learn that the easy way—through trust—or the hard way—through wandering. I've tasted both. And I can say without a doubt: **obedience is the better road.**

"God doesn't focus on what we're taking from Him but on what we're taking from ourselves."

5

MALACHI 3:10—THE ONLY TIME GOD SAYS "TEST ME"

There's a moment in Scripture that should stop every reader in their tracks.

Malachi 3:10.

It's the only place in the entire Bible where God issues a direct challenge to humanity—not a warning, not a correction, but an invitation:

"Test Me in this."

This isn't a casual suggestion. It's a divine dare. A holy challenge issued not out of frustration, but out of love and longing—a Father asking His children to try Him, to trust Him, and to see what He is capable of doing.

Let's look at the passage:

Malachi 3:6-12 (NIV)

6 "I, the Lord, do not change. So you, the descendants of Jacob, are not destroyed. 7 Ever since the time of your ancestors, you have turned away from my decrees and have not kept them. Return to me, and I will return to you," says the Lord Almighty. "But you ask, 'How are we to return?'" 8 "Will a mere mortal rob God? Yet you rob me." "But you ask, 'How are we robbing you?'" "In tithes and offerings. 9 You are under a curse—your whole nation—because you are robbing me." 10 "Bring the whole tithe into the storehouse, that there may be food in my house. Test me in this," says the Lord Almighty, "and see if I will not throw open the floodgates of heaven and pour out so much blessing that there will not be room enough to store it." 11 "I will prevent pests from devouring your crops, and the vines in your fields will not drop their fruit before it is ripe," says the Lord Almighty. 12 "Then all the nations will call you blessed, for yours will be a delightful land," says the Lord Almighty."

The Context That Changes Everything

To understand the weight of this challenge, we need to understand the historical moment. The Israelites had returned from Babylonian exile. The temple had been rebuilt. Religious activity had resumed. On the surface, everything looked normal—people were worshipping, priests were serving, sacrifices were being offered.

But something was fundamentally wrong.

The prophet Malachi was writing to a people who had grown spiritually complacent. They weren't outright rebels—they were worse. They were religious people who had lost their passion for God. They were going through the motions while their hearts drifted toward other priorities.

Sound familiar?

This is the condition of much of the American church today. We attend services, sing the songs, know the right answers, but our checkbooks reveal where our hearts really are. We've become experts at religious activity while remaining amateurs at spiritual surrender.

The people in Malachi's day were bringing offerings, but they were bringing their leftovers. Blemished animals. Damaged goods. The equivalent of throwing loose change in the offering plate while spending hundreds on entertainment, thousands on vacations, and tens of thousands on luxury items.

God's response through Malachi is both heartbreaking and hopeful. He doesn't abandon them. He doesn't write them off. Instead, He issues the most extraordinary challenge in all of Scripture.

What's happening here?

The people hadn't abandoned religion. They were still bringing offerings, still attending the temple. But their hearts had grown distant. They were giving some—but not all. Their generosity was partial. Sporadic. Convenient.

And God calls it what it is: robbery.

That might seem harsh... until we realize what's really being stolen. God doesn't need our money. What He desires is our trust. Our first. Our faith. And when we withhold the tithe, it's not just dollars we're keeping—it's the opportunity to partner with Him in blessing the world, and to live in the flow of His provision.

The Hebrew word for "rob" here is *qaba*, which means to overreach, to defraud, or to take what belongs to another. This isn't petty theft—it's systematic embezzlement. When we withhold the tithe, we're not just being stingy; we're taking what was never ours to begin with.

But here's what moves me most about this passage: God doesn't focus on what we're taking from Him. He focuses on what we're taking from ourselves. The curse isn't punishment—it's a natural consequence. When we try to keep what belongs to God, we forfeit the blessing that comes from partnership with Him.

Think about it this way: if you discovered that your financial advisor was skimming 10% off your investments, you wouldn't just be angry about the money. You'd be devastated about the lost opportunity—the compound growth, the potential returns, the future security that was stolen not just from your account, but from your family's future.

That's what's happening when we withhold the tithe. We're not just robbing God of what belongs to Him—we're robbing ourselves of the blessing that comes from obedience. We're stealing from our own spiritual growth, our own peace of mind, our own opportunity to see God work miracles in our finances.

To help myself grasp what God was expressing, I imagined it this way:

Picture building a business from scratch. You invest blood, sweat, and tears to launch it. You provide the vision, the structure, the product, and the customers. Eventually, you hand over the day-to-day management to trusted leaders. You keep supplying the resources—opportunity, tools, ideas—but you ask them to steward it well and return the first 10% so that you can continue growing, expanding, and blessing more through the work.

But then, the managers start holding back.

First, they give less than agreed. Then they delay it. Eventually, they give nothing at all.

Not because they're evil. Just distracted. Focused on other things.

And now, the initiatives you planned—the people you wanted to help, the growth you envisioned—are stalled. Not because you lack resources, but because your trusted partners won't return what was never theirs to keep.

Now add another layer. What if those stewards were your own children?

What if the 10% wasn't just for business, but was going to be used to invite them into something greater than they imagined—impact, purpose, legacy, fulfillment?

You wouldn't just be angry. You'd be heartbroken.

That's the image I see in Malachi. A Father, heartbroken, not because we've failed to follow a rule, but because we're missing out on the joy of partnering with Him.

This illustration helped me understand why God's language in Malachi is so emotionally charged. This isn't divine anger—it's divine grief. God isn't mad that we're not following rules; He's heartbroken that we're missing out on a relationship. He's not disappointed in our performance; He's devastated that we're forfeiting our own blessing.

The business analogy also reveals something crucial about how God views our resources. We tend to think of our income as something we've earned through our own effort. But God sees it as something He's provided through our partnership with Him. We bring the effort; He brings the opportunity. We bring the talent; He brings the platform. We bring the work; He brings the results.

When we withhold the tithe, we're essentially saying, "I did this on my own. I don't need you as a partner. I can handle my finances without your input." This isn't just disobedience—it's a declaration of independence from the very One who made our success possible in the first place.

The Test That Reveals God's Heart

Most of the time, we are the ones being tested. But here?

God flips the script.

He says:

"Test Me. Try Me. Let me show My faithfulness to you."

This test isn't about proving our devotion.

It's about discovering His faithfulness.

The Hebrew word for "test" here is *bachan*, which means to examine, to prove, or to try. It's the same word used for testing metals to determine their purity or testing materials to verify their strength. God is essentially saying, "Put Me to the test. See if I'm really who I claim to be. Examine My faithfulness. Prove My character."

This is stunning when you think about it. The God of the universe—the One who spoke galaxies into existence, who holds the seas in the palm of His hand, who numbers every hair on our heads—is willing to be tested by His own creation. He's so confident in His ability to provide that He welcomes our skepticism and invites our experimentation.

But notice what He asks us to test Him with: the tithe. Not prayer, not worship, not service—though all of these are important. He specifically challenges us to test Him through our finances. Why? Because He knows that our money reveals our heart like nothing else. How we handle our resources exposes our deepest beliefs about His character, His provision, and His faithfulness.

The test isn't whether God will pass—He always does. The test is whether we're willing to take it. Are we brave enough to find out what God can do when we trust Him with our finances? Are we courageous enough to discover what His faithfulness looks like in our bank accounts?

This is what makes the tithe so terrifying and so thrilling. It's not just about giving money; it's about giving God permission to prove Himself in the most practical area of our lives. It's about creating space for Him to demonstrate His power in our paychecks, our bills, our savings, and our spending.

The Promise That Defies Logic

God's promise in response to our test is almost too good to believe:

"I will throw open the floodgates of heaven and pour out so much blessing that there will not be room enough to store it."

The imagery here is overwhelming. This isn't a trickle or a steady stream—it's a flood. The Hebrew word for "pour out" is *riyq*, which means to empty completely, to pour out until the container is empty. God is saying He will empty heaven's storehouse of blessings into our lives.

But what kind of blessing is He promising? Many people immediately think of financial blessing, and while that's certainly included, God's promise is much broader. The Hebrew word for blessing here is *berakah*, which encompasses prosperity, favor, peace, protection, and divine enablement.

Notice that God doesn't promise to make us rich—He promises to make us blessed. There's a significant difference. Riches can be lost, stolen, or destroyed. Blessing is a state of divine favor that transcends circumstances. You can be financially wealthy but spiritually poor. You can have little money but be incredibly blessed.

God's promise includes financial provision, but it's not limited to it. He promises to prevent pests from devouring our crops—to protect what we have. He promises that our vines won't drop their fruit before it's ripe, to ensure that our efforts produce lasting results. He promises that other nations will call us blessed, to give us a reputation for divine favor.

The promise is both practical and spiritual, both immediate and eternal. God commits to providing for our needs, protecting our resources, and establishing our reputation as people who live under His blessing. This isn't just about having more money—it's about living in such obvious divine favor that others can't help but notice.

My Personal Laboratory

And let me say this plainly: I have lived this at Tithe Lending and Tithe Foundation.

The journey of building those ventures has been soaked in this principle. At times, we gave when it felt risky. We tithed before the bottom line made sense. We placed first things first—even when it cost us or when we couldn't see clearly what was coming next.

And again and again, God proved true to His word.

Let me share some specific examples of how this has played out in our business:

A Faith-Filled Timeline: When we first launched Tithe Lending, we committed to tithing from our very first dollar of revenue. Any accountant or business planner would have thought we were crazy. "Wait until you're profitable," would have been sound business advice. "Build up some reserves first." But we knew that if we waited until it felt safe, we'd never do it. So we started tithing immediately, even when it meant income sacrifice for our ownership. We were dedicated to the surrender and the peace that came with tithing.

Within six months, we had seen God move in ways that we didn't imagine. We began seeing profitable months on the P&L when our industry was losing money as a whole. Referrals started to come from sources we'd never contacted. Deals that should have fallen through somehow came together. We were operating in a realm of provision that defied our business plan. We weren't without challenges, but God carried us through. That initial willingness to step forward in faith paid off, and we all became closer to God as a result.

The Unexpected Partnerships: In our second year, we began to get calls and emails from other Christian business leaders. They were interested in how our journey was playing out. They were also interested in joining in on our mission of loving our neighbors in need. Within 12 months, we executed over twenty partnerships for the Tithe Foundation. Each business or leader signed a pledge dedicating their business to the Lord and setting aside at least 10% of company profits for Kingdom causes.

Our leap of faith and dedication to operating on God's principles became the catalyst for others' courage. We didn't see that coming. God began to work in and through us in new ways beyond our vision. Not only was that incredible to experience, but it was way more fun! Solo giving and solo missions can be impactful, but there is something different about running along-side other members of the Body of Christ. Together, we are more impactful. The momentum we experience is compounded. God provided additional joy that we could not have anticipated.

The Multiplication Effect: Perhaps most remarkably, we've discovered that our tithe often produces returns that exceed expectations. In 2024, our tithe represented over 62% of our company profits. By conventional business wisdom, that should have crippled us. Instead, it's been the foundation of our growth. The more we give, the more God provides opportunities to give.

This isn't just about money—it's about the peace that comes from operating in God's favor. When you know you're honoring God with your finances, you sleep better. You worry less. You make decisions with confidence because you know you're aligned with His will.

The Ripple Effect: The blessing of tithing extends far beyond our own business. Because we tithe, we've been able to fund ministries that are reaching people we'll never meet. We've supported churches that are planting new congregations. We've contributed to Christian schools that are shaping the next generation. Our tithe has become a rock thrown into the pond of God's kingdom, creating ripples that will extend into eternity.

We've seen provisions that we couldn't have manufactured.

We've watched doors open that no hustle could force.

We've experienced a peace and clarity that no business plan could produce.

The testing of God through tithing has become more than a financial principle for us—it's become a way of life. We've learned to trust God not just with our money, but with our business decisions, our hiring choices, our marketing strategies, and our long-term vision. The tithe was the gateway to a deeper level of dependence on God in every area of our operation.

The Invitation Still Stands

God already knows His plan. He doesn't ask us to test Him for His sake. He asks us to test Him for ours.

He wants to show you what He can do—if you'll only trust Him.

This invitation isn't just for business owners or high earners. It's for everyone. Whether you're making $30,000 or $300,000, whether you're a student or a retiree, whether you're single or married with kids—God's challenge remains the same: "Test Me in this."

The beauty of this test is that it's completely accessible. You don't need special training or unique qualifications. You don't need to understand complex theological concepts or master ancient languages. You just need to be willing to trust God with 10% of your income and see what He does with it.

But here's what I've learned: the test isn't really about the money. It's about the heart. God isn't looking for your cash—He's looking for your trust. He's not interested in your wallet—He's interested in your worship. The tithe is simply the vehicle He uses to reveal the depth of your faith and the authenticity of your surrender.

When you test God through tithing, you're not just discovering His faithfulness—you're discovering your own capacity for trust. You're learning that obedience leads to blessing, that surrender leads to provision, and that putting God first doesn't diminish your life—it multiplies it.

The test of tithing has the power to transform every aspect of your life. It starts with your finances, but it doesn't end there. When you learn to trust God with your money, you begin to trust Him with your career, your relationships, your health, your family, and your future.

The tithe becomes a gateway to a deeper level of faith. It's a practical demonstration of theological truth. It's a tangible expression of spiritual surrender. When you tithe, you're not just giving money—you're giving God permission to be God in your life.

When you tithe, you join a community of believers who have learned to live by faith rather than fear. You become part of a movement of people who put God's kingdom before their own comfort. You discover what it means to be truly free—not free from responsibility, but free to trust God with the outcome.

Test Him.

He knows what you need.

And He's waiting to show you that His way is always better.

The invitation stands. The challenge remains. The promise endures.

Will you take the test?

"Past miracles don't automatically produce present faith."

6

THE TEN SPIES—A TEST OF FAITH

When Moses sent twelve spies to scout out the Promised Land, the assignment was simple: explore the land and report back. But what was truly being tested wasn't their reporting skills—it was their courage and belief in God's promise. Ten of those spies came back overwhelmed by what they saw. Towering giants, fortified cities, and armies too strong for Israel to defeat. Their conclusion? "We can't do this." Only Joshua and Caleb returned with faith. Not because they saw something different, but because they believed something different.

That moment wasn't just a reconnaissance mission—it was a test. Not a test of perception, but a test of trust. God had already promised the land. The question wasn't Can they take it—it was Would they believe Him enough to act.

The ten spies failed that test, and as a result, an entire generation wandered and withered in the wilderness, not because of poor strategy or weakness, but because of unbelief. Their vision was clear, but their faith was clouded.

That same kind of test still happens today.

To understand the magnitude of this test, we need to understand the context. The Israelites were camped at Kadesh Barnea, literally on the doorstep of everything God had promised them. They had witnessed miracle after miracle—the ten plagues in Egypt, the parting of the Red Sea, manna from heaven, water from rocks. They had heard God's voice at Mount Sinai and seen His glory in the cloud by day and fire by night.

This wasn't a people lacking evidence of God's power. These were people who had front-row seats to the greatest display of divine intervention in human history. They had every reason to trust God's promises because they had personally experienced His faithfulness over and over again.

But here's what's sobering about the human heart: past miracles don't automatically produce present faith. Yesterday's victories don't guarantee today's courage. We can witness God's power and still doubt His provision. We can experience His faithfulness and still question His ability to handle our current circumstances.

The twelve spies all saw the same things. They all walked the same roads, measured the same cities, and observed the same people. But their interpretation of what they saw revealed the condition of their hearts. Ten spies saw obstacles. Two spies saw opportunities. Ten spies saw problems too big for God. Two spies saw a God too big for any problem.

This is the same challenge we face when considering tithing. We all see the same bank account balance. We all have the same monthly expenses. We all face the same economic realities. But our response to God's command to tithe reveals whether we see obstacles or opportunities, whether we trust our calculations or His promises.

The Report That Revealed Everything

When the spies returned, their report was technically accurate but spiritually devastating. Numbers 13:27-28 records their words: "We went into the land to which you sent us, and it does flow with milk and honey! Here is its fruit. But the people who live there are powerful, and the cities are fortified and very large. We even saw descendants of Anak there."

Notice the structure of their report: one sentence of God's promise fulfilled, followed by three sentences of human impossibility. Yes, the land was everything God said it would be—flowing with milk and honey, abundant with fruit. But (and that "but" changed everything) the people were too strong, the cities too fortified, the giants too intimidating.

The ten spies weren't lying. There really were giants in the land. The cities really were fortified. The armies really were powerful. But they made a crucial error: they measured God's promise against human obstacles instead of measuring human obstacles against God's power.

This is exactly what happens when we evaluate tithing. We look at our income, subtract our expenses, and conclude there's no room for a tithe. We measure God's command against our budget instead of measuring our budget against God's provision. We focus on what we can see instead of what God has said.

But listen to Joshua and Caleb's response in Numbers 13:30: "We should go up and take possession of the land, for we can certainly do it." Same facts, different faith. Same obstacles, different perspective. Same challenges, different confidence.

The difference wasn't in their circumstances—it was in their conviction about God's character.

The result of the ten spies' report was catastrophic. The entire nation believed their assessment and refused to enter the Promised Land. God's response was swift and severe: that entire generation would wander in the wilderness for forty years until they died. Only Joshua and Caleb would live to see the promise fulfilled.

Think about the tragedy of this moment. An entire generation forfeited their destiny because they believed what they could see more than what God had said. They died in the wilderness not because God was unfaithful, but because they were unbelieving. They missed their inheritance not because it wasn't available, but because they weren't willing to trust God enough to claim it.

This isn't just ancient history—it's a contemporary warning. How many believers today are wandering in a wilderness of financial anxiety because they're afraid to trust God with their money? How many are living below their spiritual inheritance because they can't bring themselves to tithe? How many are missing out on God's blessing because they trust their spreadsheets more than His promises?

The wilderness wasn't a punishment—it was a natural consequence. When we choose to live by what we can see instead of what God has said, we inevitably end up in a place of spiritual barrenness. We may have our savings accounts intact, but our souls shrivel. We may keep our money, but we lose our peace.

The tithe—returning the first tenth of our increase to God—is not just about money. It's a faith test. Will we believe God's promise to provide? Will we trust Him even when the numbers on the spreadsheet don't line up? Or will we let what we see with our eyes override what God has already spoken?

It's easy to act in strength when you have all the resources and everything adds up. But walking by faith means stepping forward when it doesn't. Today, that kind of faith is rare. Normal has become self-reliance, careful calculation, and complete control. But faith doesn't wait for full understanding.

The tithing test reveals the same spiritual dynamics that were at work at Kadesh Barnea. We can see our financial obligations stretching out before us like fortified cities. We can feel the pressure of our monthly expenses looming like giants. We can calculate the impossibility of making it work mathematically, like the ten spies calculated their military disadvantage.

But God is asking us the same question He asked Israel: Will you trust My promise or your perception? Will you believe my word or your worries? Will you step forward in faith or retreat in fear?

If you're reading this, chances are you know your personal balance sheet. You know what comes in, and you know what needs to go out. You may have even run the math and found that tithing doesn't "work" on paper. That's okay. God sees that. In fact, He anticipates it. That's why in Malachi 3:10 He invites us—commands us—to test Him because He knows that our test of Him is really a test of our faith.

The beauty of the tithing test is that it's perfectly designed to expose our true beliefs about God's character. When we withhold the tithe because we're afraid we won't have enough, we're essentially saying we don't trust God to provide. When we delay tithing until we feel more financially secure, we're declaring that our security comes from our savings account rather than our Savior.

But when we tithe despite our fears, when we give the first tenth, even when the math doesn't work, when we honor God with our resources before we pay our bills— we're making the same declaration of faith that Joshua and Caleb made: "Our God is bigger than our obstacles."

My Kadesh Barnea Moment

I can remember the defining moment in my life when this truth became personal. I was preparing to launch a mortgage company called "Tithe" at a time when profit margins in the industry didn't come anywhere near 10%. It seemed like madness. Friends, peers, and even mentors questioned the logic. And if I'm honest, so did I. From the outside looking in, it looked foolish. Risky. Destined for failure.

The mortgage industry operates on razor-thin margins. Most companies are thrilled to achieve a 3-4% profit margin. Many operate at break-even or loss for years while building market share. The idea of giving away 10% of gross revenue—not profit, but revenue—before paying salaries, rent, or any other expenses seemed financially suicidal.

I spent countless hours running projections, stress-testing scenarios, and trying to make the numbers work. Every financial model I created suggested the same conclusion: this approach was unsustainable. The mathematical giants in the land seemed too formidable to overcome.

But something deeper was stirring in my heart. I knew God was calling me to step into this venture, not despite the financial impossibility, but because of it. He wanted to demonstrate His faithfulness in a way that would leave no doubt about the source of our success. He wanted our story to become a testimony to His provision, not a monument to our business acumen.

So I sat down with a spiritual mentor who had walked with me through that season, and seasons since. I shared my concerns, the numbers, the fear. And he asked me a question I'll never forget—one that I now ask others when they face their own test of faith.

"What is the opposite of faith?"

Like many, I answered quickly: "Fear." Others might say "doubt." Both answers seem reasonable. They certainly reflect resistance to faith. But over the years, I've come to see it differently.

The true opposite of faith isn't fear.

It's assurance.

When you have full assurance of an outcome, faith is no longer needed. Hebrews 11:1 defines faith this way: "Now faith is confidence in what we hope for and assurance about what we do not see."

Faith exists precisely because we don't have all the answers. It lives in the gap between what we see and what we know God has said. That's where God meets us. That's where trust is built.

This revelation transformed my understanding of the tithing test. I had been waiting for assurance—for the math to work out, for the margins to improve, for the fear to subside. But God wasn't asking me to wait for assurance. He was asking me to step forward in faith, precisely because I didn't have all the answers.

Fear, I realized, wasn't the enemy of faith—it was often the companion of faith. The disciples were afraid when Jesus called them to leave their nets, but they followed anyway. Abraham was probably terrified when God asked him to sacrifice Isaac, but he obeyed anyway. Moses was certainly fearful when God sent him to confront Pharaoh, but he went anyway.

The presence of fear doesn't disqualify us from walking by faith. In fact, it's often evidence that we're moving in the right direction. When we step beyond our ability to control outcomes, when we move past our capacity to guarantee results, when we venture into territory that requires divine intervention—that's when faith becomes necessary.

Assurance eliminates the need for faith because it eliminates risk. But faith thrives in the realm of risk, in the space between promise and fulfillment, in the gap between calling and completion.

The Step That Changes Everything

When I stepped forward to start the company, fear and doubt were real—but so was the leading of the Holy Spirit. I couldn't explain it. I couldn't predict the outcome. But I knew I was supposed to move. And in doing so, I learned that fear isn't always the enemy. Sometimes, it's a sign that you're heading in the right direction because you're no longer relying on yourself.

The decision to launch Tithe Lending while committing to tithe from day one was my Kadesh Barnea moment. I could focus on the giants in the land—the slim margins, the competitive market, the financial impossibility—or I could focus on the God who had called me into this venture.

I chose to believe that the same God who had provided for me in the corporate world could provide for me in the entrepreneurial world. The same God who had blessed my previous business endeavors could bless this one. The same God who had promised to provide for those who put Him first could be trusted with my financial future.

But here's what I discovered: God often waits for that step of faith before He reveals the next thing. He doesn't show us the entire staircase before asking us to take the first step. He doesn't provide a detailed business plan before calling us to trust Him. He invites us to walk with Him, not just to wait until the path is fully lit.

The first year of Tithe Lending was a master class in divine provision. Doors opened that we never knocked on. Clients appeared that we never solicited. Opportunities emerged that we never pursued. It was as if God was saying, "You trusted Me with your first fruits, now watch what I can do with the rest."

After our second year, our tithe represented 62% of our profits, by conventional business standards, which should have been devastating. Instead, it was liberating. We were operating in a realm where God's economics superseded earthly economics, where His provision transcended human calculation.

The Caleb and Joshua Spirit

God often waits for that step of faith before He reveals the next thing. He invites us to walk with Him, not just to wait until the path is fully lit. Because it's in the walking, the trusting, and the risking that our relationship with Him grows deeper. Each step, no matter how small, becomes a place where His presence meets us—and where our faith becomes more than just theory.

So be like Caleb and Joshua. Not because they were fearless, but because they believed God was greater than what they saw. Don't let your own strength—or lack thereof—determine what's possible. Don't stay stuck in the wilderness of indecision, paralyzed by numbers, logic, or fear. Step forward in faith, even if your hands are trembling.

Caleb and Joshua weren't superhuman. They felt the same fear as the other ten spies. They saw the same giants, the same fortified cities, the same overwhelming obstacles. But they had learned something the others hadn't: God's promises are more reliable than human perception.

When Caleb said, "We should go up and take possession of the land, for we can certainly do it," he wasn't speaking from mathematical certainty. He was speaking from theological conviction. He wasn't calculating probability; he was declaring possibility.

This is the spirit we need when facing the tithing test. We need the audacity to believe that God's promise to provide is more trustworthy than our budget projections. We need the courage to act on His word even when our bank account seems inadequate. We need the faith to give the first tenth even when we can't see how the remaining ninety percent will cover our needs.

The Caleb and Joshua spirit isn't about being reckless with money—it's about being faithful with trust. It's not about ignoring financial realities—it's about believing that God's reality is bigger than financial limitations.

The Wilderness Alternative

The test of the ten spies wasn't just for them—it's for us too. Will we trust what God says over what we see? Will we walk into the unknown, believing that His promises are still true?

The alternative to faith is the wilderness. Not necessarily a geographical wilderness, but a spiritual one. It's the place where we exist between promise and fulfillment, between calling and completion, between potential and actualization.

The wilderness isn't always a place of suffering—sometimes it's a place of safety. It's comfortable. Predictable. Manageable. We know what to expect. We can control our environment. We can calculate our outcomes.

But the wilderness is also a place of limitation. Nothing grows there. Nothing multiplies there. Nothing flourishes there. We may survive in the wilderness, but we don't thrive. We may remain in the wilderness, but we don't advance.

Many believers spend their entire lives in a financial wilderness, afraid to trust God with their money, afraid to step into the promised land of tithing, afraid to discover what God might do if they put Him first in their finances.

The tragedy is that the wilderness is optional. God's promises are available to every believer. His provision is accessible to every follower. His blessing is within reach of every faithful steward. But we must be willing to leave the wilderness of fear and enter the promised land of faith.

Scary moments will come. But the presence of fear doesn't mean the absence of God. Let the Holy Spirit guide you. Let God's word steady you. And believe this: you can walk by faith. Not because you're fearless, but because you trust the One who goes with you.

The test of faith doesn't end when we start tithing—it deepens. Each month when the tithe is due, we face the same choice Joshua and Caleb faced: Will we trust God's promise or our perception? Will we act on His word or our worries?

But here's what I've discovered: each act of faith makes the next one easier. Each time we choose to trust God with our finances, our confidence in His provision grows. Each month we tithe faithfully, we accumulate evidence of His faithfulness.

The test of faith becomes a lifestyle of faith. The single act of obedience becomes a pattern of dependence. The initial step of trust becomes a journey of intimacy with the One who provides for all our needs.

This is why tithing is so much more than a financial transaction—it's a spiritual transformation. It changes not just our giving, but our living. It affects not just our wallets, but our worship. It influences not just our money, but our entire relationship with God.

The test continues. The promise endures. The choice is yours.

"We adapt to blessings so quickly that we forget it was ever a blessing at all."

7

THE TEN LEPERS—A TEST OF GRATITUDE

In Luke 17, Jesus encounters ten men afflicted with leprosy—outcasts, isolated, and desperate for healing. With a word, He restores them. Ten lives transformed in an instant. But then something shocking happens: only one returns to thank Him.

Just one.

All ten were physically healed. But only one was made whole in spirit. Jesus wasn't simply performing a miracle—He was testing hearts. Would they stop to recognize the Giver, or would they take the gift and run?

This story is more than a lesson in manners. It's a piercing look into how easily we forget the source of our blessings. Gratitude isn't just a feeling—it's a posture of the heart. And in this passage, Jesus makes it clear: He's not just looking for recipients. He's looking for worshipers.

What strikes me about the nine who didn't return is that their healing was just as real, just as complete, just as miraculous as the one who came back. They weren't fake healed or partially restored. Jesus didn't withhold anything from them because of their future ingratitude. His grace was complete and unconditional.

But their response reveals something troubling about human nature: we have an incredible capacity to normalize miracles. What amazes us today becomes routine tomorrow. What seems impossible this week feels ordinary next month. We adapt to blessings so quickly that we forget it was ever a blessing at all.

Think about your own life. The fact that you woke up this morning—that's a miracle your body performed automatically. The breath in your lungs, the beat of your heart, the thoughts in your mind—all gifts you didn't earn and couldn't manufacture. Yet how often do we pause to be grateful for them?

The nine lepers represent our default spiritual condition: blessed but ungrateful, healed but hurried, recipients of grace but not recognizers of the Giver. They got what they came for and moved on with their lives, never understanding that the healing was an invitation to a relationship, not just restoration.

The Heart Behind the Healing

Tithing is one way God tests our gratitude. It's a practical, tangible way we say, "Lord, I know where this came from. I know it's Yours. Thank You." It's not about God needing our money. It's about whether we'll acknowledge Him as the source.

The beautiful thing about the one leper who returned is that his gratitude cost him something. While the other nine were presumably rushing off to show themselves to the priests, to reunite with their families, to reclaim their lives, this one stopped. He chose worship over convenience. He prioritized Thanksgiving over productivity.

This is exactly what tithing requires of us. It costs us something—not just the money, but the time to write the check, the intentionality to prioritize it, the faith to trust God with what remains. When we tithe, we're saying the same thing the grateful leper said: "Jesus, You are the source, and I won't move forward without acknowledging that."

The test of gratitude through tithing reveals what we really believe about God's role in our success. When we withhold the tithe, we're essentially saying, "I did this. This income is the result of my effort, my talent, my hard work." When we give the tithe, we're declaring, "God,

You are the source of every good gift, and I worship You with what You've given me."

And here's the truth: when we withhold our tithe, we may still enjoy blessings. The rain falls on the just and the unjust. But we miss something greater—we miss the joy of worship. The fullness of relationship. The deep, soul-level peace that comes when we give back in recognition of who He is and what He's done.

We were not created just to survive. We weren't created to accumulate. We certainly weren't made by accident. We were created in the image of God—to glorify Him and walk in relationship with Him. That is the highest calling of humanity: to know God and make Him known.

How can we possibly do that without a heart of gratitude?

Hebrews 11:3 puts it like this:

"By faith we understand that the universe was formed at God's command, so that what is seen was not made out of what was visible."

That verse hits me every time. What we see was made from what we cannot see. That means everything—our life, our breath, our resources, our opportunities—flow from the invisible hand of a generous God. He is the source. Always has been.

When we give thanks, when we tithe, we aren't just following a rule—we're aligning ourselves with reality. We're saying, "God, You made all of this. You sustain all of this. And I worship You with what You've given."

That kind of giving is no longer about duty. It becomes an overflow of worship. A natural response to the generosity of the Creator who didn't have to make us, but did. Who didn't have to bless you, but does. Who didn't have to invite us into His mission—but has.

The One Who Made the Difference

What made the tenth leper different wasn't his level of desperation—they were all desperate. It wasn't his degree of need—they all had the same disease. It wasn't even his amount of faith—Jesus healed all ten based on their collective faith.

The difference was his response to the blessing. While nine saw healing as an end, one saw it as a beginning. While nine viewed the miracle as a solution to their problem, one understood it as an invitation to a relationship.

This is the heart posture that tithing cultivates in us. When we regularly give back to God, we train ourselves to see His hand in our provision. We develop eyes to recognize His faithfulness. We build a rhythm of gratitude that transforms not just our giving, but our living.

The grateful leper didn't just receive healing—he received a deeper revelation of who Jesus was. His gratitude opened his heart to experience not just the power of God, but the presence of God. His worship didn't just acknowledge the miracle—it encountered the miracle-worker.

This is what we miss when we fail to tithe: not just the blessing that comes from obedience, but the relationship that comes from recognition. Not just the financial provision that follows faithfulness, but the spiritual intimacy that flows from gratitude.

Let us not be like the nine who walked away healed, yet unchanged in spirit. Let us be like the one who turned back, fell at Jesus' feet, and gave thanks. Let our tithe be a testimony—not just of obedience, but of overflowing gratitude for a God who gives so freely and loves so deeply.

"Tithing plays a quiet
but powerful role in that
spiritual readiness."

8

THE TEN VIRGINS—A TEST OF READINESS

In Matthew 25, Jesus tells a striking parable about ten virgins awaiting the arrival of the bridegroom. All ten start in the same place—waiting with anticipation. But only five bring extra oil, prepared for a delay. The others, caught off guard when the bridegroom finally arrives, find themselves shut out of the wedding feast.

This isn't just a story about oil or lamps—it's about spiritual readiness. The parable reminds us that following Jesus isn't only about how we start. It's about how we continue. It's about staying awake, staying filled, staying faithful—until the very end.

What's sobering about this parable is how similar the ten virgins appeared on the surface. They all had lamps. They all had some oil. They all claimed to be ready for the bridegroom's arrival. From the outside, you couldn't tell the difference between the wise and the foolish.

But when the crisis came, when the oil ran out, when the bridegroom was delayed longer than expected— that's when the difference became clear. The foolish virgins had enough oil for the short term, but not enough for the long haul. They were prepared for convenience, but not for cost.

This perfectly illustrates the difference between cultural Christianity and committed discipleship. Many people appear spiritually ready on Sunday morning, but the test comes Monday through Saturday. The question isn't whether we can maintain our spiritual appearance for a few hours—it's whether we can sustain our spiritual reality for a lifetime.

Tithing is one of those practices that separates appearance from reality. It's easy to look spiritual in a church service when you're not asked to sacrifice anything. It's simple to appear generous when generosity costs you nothing. But when the offering plate is passed, when the tithe is due, when your resources are on the line—that's when your true spiritual condition is revealed.

Tithing plays a quiet but powerful role in that spiritual readiness. When we tithe, we do more than give money—we shape our hearts. We build a rhythm of putting God first. With each tithe, we say, "Jesus, I'm living for You and Your Kingdom. I'm not living for myself." It's a regular declaration that our lives are aligned with eternity, not with temporary things.

This kind of readiness isn't abstract. It's not a hypothetical test—it's our daily reality. Jesus could return at any moment. Or we could step into eternity at any moment. Life moves forward moment by moment, and while we don't know when our final moment will be, we know it's coming.

The wise virgins weren't just prepared for the bridegroom's arrival—they were prepared for his delay. They understood that readiness isn't a one-time decision but an ongoing discipline. They brought extra oil because they knew that waiting well requires resources.

Tithing serves as our spiritual "extra oil." It's not just about being obedient in the moment—it's about building spiritual muscle that can sustain us through seasons of delay, difficulty, and testing. Each time we tithe, we're making a deposit in our spiritual readiness account.

The Battle for Attention

What makes readiness difficult today is not just sin—it's distraction. The sheer volume of noise in modern life numbs our spiritual awareness. According to The Times, the average American spends roughly 2.5 hours per day on social media. Teenagers spend even more, nearly 5 hours per day. Add to that the average 2 hours a day watching television (with those over 65 watching over 4 hours daily), and we're looking at over 31 hours per week of screen-based media. That's the equivalent of more than 68 full 24-hour days each year—over two months spent consuming content instead of cultivating life.

This isn't harmless background noise—it shapes us. It builds a rhythm, but one designed to distract, dull, and disconnect us from God. Left unchecked, this rhythm draws our attention away from what matters most and slowly erodes our readiness.

The foolish virgins weren't necessarily rebellious—they were simply unprepared. They didn't plan for the long term. They didn't consider what would happen if things didn't go as expected. They lived for the moment instead of the mission.

Modern distraction works the same way. It doesn't usually pull us into outright sin—it just pulls us away from spiritual intentionality. We don't become enemies of God; we just become distracted from God. We don't reject Jesus; we just forget to prepare for His return.

The Counter-Rhythm of Faith

Tithing cuts through that noise. It establishes a counter-rhythm—one of surrender, priority, and trust. Most of us receive income on a consistent schedule. Tithing aligns that routine with divine purpose. It turns a paycheck into a spiritual practice. It takes something ordinary and infuses it with eternal significance.

When we tithe regularly, we create a monthly reminder that this life is temporary and eternity is permanent. We establish a rhythm that says, "God first" before we pay any other bill. We build a practice that prioritizes the kingdom of heaven over the kingdoms of this world.

The wise virgins didn't just happen to be ready— they prepared to be ready. They thought ahead. They planned for contingencies. They brought extra oil not because they were worried, but because they were wise.

Tithing is our way of bringing "extra oil" to our spiritual life. It's a discipline that prepares us for the long obedience of following Jesus. It's a practice that builds our spiritual endurance for the marathon of faith.

Will tithing alone make every part of your life spiritually ready? Of course not. But it's a step that invites more of God into your life. It's a discipline that disrupts worldly monotony and creates space for holy awareness. It's a practical act of devotion in a world full of distractions.

The tragic irony of the foolish virgins is that they were so close to the wedding feast. They had been waiting. They had been anticipating. They had their lamps and their oil. But when the moment came, they weren't ready.

How many believers today are spiritually close but practically unprepared? How many are culturally

Christian but not deeply committed? How many appear ready on the surface but lack the spiritual reserves to sustain them when testing comes?

The test of readiness through tithing isn't about perfection—it's about preparation. It's about building spiritual habits that will sustain us not just in good times, but in hard times. Not just when faith is easy, but when faith is costly.

Let's not be caught unprepared. Let's be like the wise virgins, whose lamps were full and whose hearts were ready. Let's live lives that declare: "Jesus, I know You are coming—and I'm living like it."

Let's pass the test of readiness—not by accident, but by intention.

PART 2

" ───────────────────────

"We start thinking we're

pursuing success, but we end

up being pursued by it."

"

9

FROM EMPTINESS TO PURPOSE

Before I understood the heart behind tithing, my life was a constant chase after moving targets. I was keeping 100% of my earnings for my purposes while thinking mostly about my personal journey and the things I wanted. The problem with living inside my subjective point of view was that what I wanted was constantly changing. The world around me was shifting. New targets would emerge not just annually, but monthly.

New cars and body styles roll out each year. New homes are intriguing when they're in areas you'd rather spend time in. New vacations always seem to be the answer to unwind. New work goals seem to rise and fall with an ever-changing market and a constant need to compete. Most of my goals revolved around growth for the sake of it, especially at work.

Looking back, I realize I had fallen into what I now call the "success trap"—the belief that achievement equals fulfillment, that accumulation equals abundance, that climbing higher always means living better. This trap is particularly dangerous because it's reinforced by everything around us. Our culture celebrates the climb. Our economy rewards accumulation. Our social media feeds showcase the achievements.

But what no one tells you about the success trap is how isolating it becomes. The higher you climb, the fewer people understand your struggles. The more you achieve, the more pressure you feel to achieve even more. The more you accumulate, the more you worry about protecting what you have. Success, as I had defined it, became a prison with golden bars.

The mortgage industry was perfectly designed to feed this trap. Every month brought new loan volume targets. Every quarter demanded higher profit margins. Every year, there is an expanded market share. There was always another mountain to climb, another competitor to beat, another milestone to reach. And for a while, I thrived in that environment because I genuinely believed that bigger was always better, that more was always the answer.

But somewhere along the way, the victories started feeling hollow. The bonuses lost their excitement. The recognition felt empty. I was winning by every external measure while dying by every internal one.

As President of a large financial institution, growth was something I was used to aiming at. If you're not growing, you're dying... and I still agree with that. The issue with certain types of growth is not tactics or pursuits, but our reasons and purpose. Eventually, everyone wants to know why they do what they do, who it impacts beyond just numbers, and what they'll be remembered for if they complete it well. In my case, I continued to ask these questions with no certain answers.

The moving target problem is real. When your goals are driven by external circumstances rather than internal convictions, you're constantly recalibrating, constantly adjusting, constantly chasing something just out of reach. Today's achievement becomes tomorrow's starting point. This year's success becomes next year's baseline expectation.

I remember the exhausting cycle of quarterly reviews, annual planning sessions, and strategic visioning meetings. We would set ambitious targets, work frantically to hit them, celebrate briefly when we succeeded, then immediately start planning for even higher targets. There was no finish line, no moment of contentment, no sense of "enough."

This is the curse of living for goals without a greater purpose. The goals themselves become the god we serve, and gods always demand more sacrifice, more devotion, more of our lives. We start thinking we're pursuing success, but we end up being pursued by it. We believe we're in control, but we're actually being controlled.

The irony is that this kind of growth is ultimately unsustainable. You can only push harder for so long before something breaks—your health, your relationships, your sanity, or your soul. I was heading toward that breaking point, but I was too busy climbing to notice how unstable the ladder had become.

I did my job because that's what was called for. I worked hard because that's who I was. I told myself that I did it because I really cared about the customer. I told myself that my legacy would be building something "special". Really, I just lied to myself to keep it all going. In reality, what I sold was the same thing that hundreds of other companies had access to. Sure, I wanted to do a good job for the clients of our company, but no one really talked much about the customer inside our internal meetings. It was all about us, all the time. My legacy would have become building something for my own personal benefit, and selling myself that I was doing it for others. I was full of crap, and I knew it.

This might be the most painful paragraph for me to read, even now, because it captures the depth of self-deception I had perfected. I had become an expert at creating noble narratives for selfish ambitions. I could make every decision sound customer-focused, every strategy sound service-oriented, every goal sound purpose-driven.

But late at night, when the presentations were finished and the meetings were over, I knew the truth. I was building a kingdom, but it was a kingdom of one. I was serving a cause, but the cause was my own advancement. I was creating a legacy, but it was a legacy of personal achievement disguised as corporate contribution.

The mortgage industry, like many industries, makes this self-deception easy. You can convince yourself that you're helping people achieve the American dream when you're really just processing transactions. You can tell yourself that you're providing essential financial services when you're really just maximizing profit margins. You can claim to be building something meaningful when you're really just building your own reputation.

The customers became abstractions—numbers on a spreadsheet, deals in a pipeline, revenue in a forecast. We talked about customer satisfaction scores, but we weren't really concerned about customer satisfaction. We were concerned about customer acquisition, customer retention, and customer profitability. The language of service masked the reality of self-interest.

This disconnect between our stated values and our actual priorities created a constant undercurrent of cognitive dissonance. I knew what we claimed to be about, and I knew what we were actually about, and those two things didn't align. Living in that gap between image and reality was spiritually exhausting.

The Collision with Reality

This led to a deep internal struggle. I wanted more out of life. I knew I had to work. Didn't have a choice. But I no longer felt connected to my work. I felt like I was short-changing my family, so I could continue with a façade that I'd created, and didn't want it all to fall apart. At times, I wished my life would just be over. I was exhausted, afraid, and empty. This is what a life of knocking down goal after goal, paycheck after paycheck, and reward after reward had earned me. Emptiness, brokenness, and a desire for it all to end rather than being excited for where it might lead. I coped with the stress poorly. I drank. I did my best to numb the feelings of emptiness the best that I could.

The collision between external success and internal emptiness is devastating. You can't explain it to people because, from the outside, your life looks enviable. You have the title, the income, the house, the car, and the respect. What's to complain about? How can you be miserable when you have everything you thought you wanted?

But that's exactly the problem—you have everything you thought you wanted, and it's not enough. In fact, it's worse than not enough. It's actively draining. Every achievement reveals how hollow achievement really is. Every acquisition demonstrates how temporary possessions really are. Every promotion exposes how insatiable ambition really is.

The family aspect was particularly painful. I was working longer hours to provide a better life for my wife and kids, but my longer hours were actually making their lives worse. They needed my presence more than my provision, my attention more than my ambition, my heart more than my hustle. But I had convinced myself that working harder was how I showed love, that climbing higher was how I served them.

The truth is, I was afraid to stop. I was afraid that if I slowed down, everything would fall apart. I was afraid that if I stopped striving, I would lose my identity. I was afraid that if I stopped climbing, I would discover that I was actually much closer to the bottom than I thought.

So I numbed the pain instead of addressing it. Alcohol became my way of silencing the internal questions that were getting louder every day. I didn't drink because I enjoyed it—I drank because I couldn't stand being fully present in my own life. The emptiness was too loud, the meaninglessness too obvious, the futility too overwhelming.

The Moment Everything Changed

Then, God showed me another way.

I heard my first message on tithing late in 2020. Our Pastor took us on a journey one Sunday that totally unlocked what had been missing for me before. It's like my spiritual eyes were finally opened. Thank God. My work could mean so much more, but it wouldn't unless I understood the provider and master whom I served. God wasn't just after my money. He was after my heart. Not because he wanted to keep score, but because he wants to bless me. The tithe is an invitation to so much more. A life of endless meaning. A way for me to attach my temporary effort to eternal significance. It became a gateway for me to understand and know the eternal creator of the universe in a personal and unique way. By tithing, I was able to see the fruit of my labor play out in the lives of others and live under a blessing that I never thought possible.

That Sunday morning message wasn't just information—it was transformation. For the first time in years, I saw a way to bridge the gap between my work and my worship, between my career and my calling, between my success and my significance.

The revelation wasn't complicated, but it was revolutionary: God wanted to be my partner, not just my provider. He wanted to use my work, not just bless it. He wanted to multiply my efforts, not just reward them. But this partnership required something I had never offered—my first fruits, my priority, my trust.

I had been treating God like a consultant I occasionally hired for advice, when He wanted to be the CEO of my entire life. I had been giving Him my leftovers—my spare time, my extra money, my backup plans—when He wanted my first and best. The tithe wasn't about Him needing my money; it was about me needing His partnership.

What struck me most about that message was the promise of meaning. For years, I had been looking for significance in achievement, purpose in position, fulfillment in financial success. But God was offering something different—a way to make every dollar I earned, every deal I closed, every client I served into an act of worship and an investment in eternity.

The tithe became the key that unlocked a completely different way of thinking about work. Instead of working for myself and giving God the leftovers, I could work for God and trust Him with the outcome. Instead of measuring success by my own accumulation, I could measure it by God's kingdom advancement. Instead of building a legacy for myself, I could participate in building something eternal.

The Birth of a New Vision

It's why I now do what I do. The same thing I did before, under a new logo. Tithe Lending was born from the bottom of a personal pit that I was in while seemingly on top of the mountain. Honoring God has become our mission. Loving our neighbor, our tactics. Putting God first through the tithe is a discipline that has transformed our hearts and our work.

The decision to start Tithe Lending wasn't just a career change—it was a complete reorientation of my life around God's priorities. I didn't change industries; I changed my understanding of why the industry exists. I didn't change my skills; I changed my motivation for using them. I didn't change my goals; I changed my definition of success.

Honoring God as our mission meant that every business decision would be filtered through the question: "Does this bring glory to God?" Loving our neighbor as our tactics meant that every interaction with clients, partners, and employees would be guided by genuine care for their well-being, not just our bottom line.

But the most radical decision was putting God first through the tithe. This wasn't just about giving away 10% of our profits—it was about giving away 10% of our revenue, right off the top, before paying salaries, rent, or any other expenses. By conventional business wisdom, this was financial suicide. By God's economy, it was the foundation of true prosperity.

The transformation wasn't just in our business model—it was in our hearts. When you start every month by giving God the first tenth of everything that comes in, you can't help but be reminded that He's the source. When you prioritize His kingdom before your own operations, you can't help but trust His provision. When you make worship the foundation of your work, you can't help but find meaning in every transaction.

What I discovered is that God doesn't just want to be included in our success—He wants to be the architect of it. When we put Him first through tithing, we're not just giving Him a portion of our resources; we're inviting Him to multiply our efforts in ways we never could have imagined.

At Tithe Lending, we've seen this multiplication happen over and over again. Clients we never solicited. Referrals we never requested. Opportunities we never pursued. It's as if God takes our faithful stewardship of the first tenth and uses it to open doors for the remaining ninety percent that no amount of marketing or networking could have opened.

But the multiplication isn't just financial—it's spiritual. When you know that your work is contributing to God's kingdom, every deal becomes meaningful.

When you understand that your success is advancing His purposes, every achievement becomes significant. When you realize that your tithe is feeding the hungry, housing the homeless, and spreading the Gospel, every dollar you earn becomes an act of worship.

The emptiness that once characterized my work has been replaced by purpose. The meaninglessness that once plagued my achievements has been transformed into significance. The isolation that once defined my success has been exchanged for partnership with the Creator of the universe.

This is what God wants for every believer—not just business owners, but every person who works, earns, and gives. He wants to transform our understanding of work from a necessary evil into a holy calling. He wants to change our relationship with money from a source of anxiety into a tool of worship. He wants to turn our careers from platforms for self-promotion into opportunities for kingdom advancement.

The tithe is the gateway to this transformation. It's the key that unlocks a life of purpose, meaning, and divine partnership. It's the discipline that converts earthly labor into eternal investment. It's the practice that transforms success from a destination into a stewardship.

From emptiness to purpose—this is the journey that tithing makes possible, not just for me, but for anyone willing to put God first and trust Him with the outcome.

"

"Time after time, we've seen

doors open that no amount

of networking or marketing

could have forced."

"

10

STORIES OF SUPERNATURAL PROVISION

The journey of building Tithe Lending has been filled with moments that can only be explained by God's supernatural intervention. When we committed to tithing 10% of our revenue before paying ourselves, we opened the door for God to work in ways that defied business logic.

Time after time, we've seen doors open that no amount of networking or marketing could have forced. Clients have come to us through connections so unlikely that we could only attribute them to divine orchestration. Resources have appeared at exactly the moment we needed them, often through channels we never could have anticipated.

The Phone Call That Changed Everything

Two months into our journey, my co-founder and I received a call that we wouldn't have believed if we didn't experience it for ourselves.

After leaving our corporate positions, we were facing a tough industry outlook in mortgage due to rising rates and low home affordability. Refinance opportunities were waning. Companies were beginning to consolidate or close, not open. Finding investors or raising debt didn't seem in the cards for us. We were prepared to bootstrap our company and pour all we had into getting it off the ground.

Little did we know, our mission and vision for Tithe Lending had made its way to a connection we'd had in prior years. A man whose heart was stirred by the Holy Spirit to provide funding for what we would build throughout 2023. We had a series of calls and agreed upon a number that would fuel the start of what God was planning for our business.

As our final call was ending, I realized I was witnessing Malachi 3:10 in real time. God had "opened the flood-gates of heaven" through a phone call from someone we'd never solicited, or even told what we were up to.

Again, if I hadn't experienced it for myself, I'm not sure I'd believe it.

But the provision came with a lesson: the call arrived only after we had honored our commitment to tithe, only after we had trusted God despite our circumstances, only after we had chosen faith over fear. He met us on the road of faith, and he has continued to do so ever since.

The Team That Built Itself

Perhaps even more remarkable than financial provision has been the supernatural way our team has come together. In an industry known for high turnover and cutthroat competition, we've assembled a group of people who share not just professional competence but spiritual alignment.

One example is our operations leader. She had been praying for a job that would allow her to use her skills while serving a higher purpose. She had never heard of Tithe Lending when she ran across a video we had posted about our mission on social media. That one impression led her to research our company, apply for a position that wasn't advertised, and ultimately join a team where she found the purpose she had been seeking.

Another example is one of our top sales leaders. He had grown disillusioned with the mortgage industry's focus on transaction volume over client care. He was actually planning to leave the field entirely. After learning about our mission, he decided to transfer his energy into pursuing not only sales but real service to those in need. Now he is in the top 1% of producers in our state. His transactions are making meaningful donations to those in need. He also uses some of his time each week to volunteer in the nonprofits that we help fund with our tithe. His work has become worship, and each transaction has become ministry fuel.

These aren't isolated incidents. Again and again, the right people have appeared at exactly the right time with exactly the right skills and, more importantly, the right heart. We've rarely had to actively recruit; instead, God has sent us team members who were already seeking what we could offer—meaningful work aligned with kingdom purposes.

The Deal That Shouldn't Have Closed

One of the day-to-day examples of supernatural provision involved a deal that encountered every possible obstacle. The borrower's income documentation was delayed, the appraisal came in lower than expected, the title search revealed an obscure lien, and the underwriter requested additional conditions just days before the scheduled closing.

By every industry standard, this deal was dead. The borrower was devastated—they had already given notice on their rental property and arranged for movers. Our team had invested dozens of hours in what now appeared to be a lost cause. The commission we had counted on for that month evaporated.

But our loan officer, driven by genuine concern for the clients, continued working the file even when conventional wisdom said to move on. He made calls that others wouldn't make, researched solutions that others wouldn't pursue, and advocated with an intensity that others wouldn't sustain.

On the morning of what should have been closing day, with everyone resigned to failure, a series of minor miracles unfolded. The delayed income documentation arrived. The seller agreed to a solution for the appraisal issues. The title company discovered that the obscure lien had actually been satisfied years earlier but never properly recorded. The underwriter, who had been busy, suddenly became available and cleared all remaining conditions within hours.

The deal closed that afternoon.

These things could all be attributed to circumstance. However, as a team, we pray to open each meeting. We pray for our clients, realtors, and vendor partners. We pray specific prayers. We pray for God to assist the families that we serve to put them in the homes that he wants to cultivate their growth through. To help our partners navigate stressful situations with grace. We pray that our efforts and care would reflect the love and concern that God has for every client we interact with. So was it all a coincidence? Maybe. But we believe that when these situations unfold in this way, they are answered prayers.

The Culture of Purpose

Our team members regularly share stories of how their work at Tithe Lending has given them a sense of purpose they never experienced in previous roles. They're not just processing loans—they're participating in a mission that honors God and serves others. This transformation in workplace culture became one of the most unexpected blessings of our tithing commitment.

One of our new employees recently told me that he had been dreading Monday mornings for years at his previous job. Now he looks forward to coming to work because he knows that every client interaction is contributing to kingdom impact through our tithe. He's not just earning a paycheck; he's participating in ministry.

This sense of purpose has practical implications beyond job satisfaction. Our team productivity consistently ranks in the top percentiles. Our client satisfaction scores remain consistently high because our people genuinely care about the outcomes.

But the most profound change is spiritual. We regularly have team members share how working at Tithe Lending has deepened their own faith, inspired their personal tithing, or clarified their understanding of how work can be worship. Some have started tithing for the first time. Others have increased their personal giving. Several have become more active in their local churches. All have a clear understanding of how their work is going farther and wider than a simple paycheck.

The ripple effect of our corporate commitment to tithing has been a team-wide transformation in how people think about money, work, and purpose. We haven't just built a profitable business; we've created a workplace ministry that impacts every person who joins our team.

Perhaps the most surprising form of supernatural provision has been the expansion of our professional network. In an industry where relationships are everything, God has connected us with people and opportunities that no amount of traditional networking could have generated.

Take our relationship with a major real estate firm in our local market. We had no prior connection to this company, no mutual contacts, and no marketing presence in their market. But one of their top agents happened to attend a retreat where Tithe was a sponsor. During a break, the agent mentioned his frustration with mortgage lenders who were all about transactions rather than relationships.

We were able to share about Tithe Lending's mission and approach. That casual conversation led to a phone call, which led to a partnership that has generated tens of thousands in revenue while serving dozens of families with integrity and excellence.

Or consider our relationship with a Christian business owner who needed creative financing. He had been working with a large bank for months with little progress. A mutual friend mentioned our commitment to tithing and kingdom impact. Intrigued, he reached out to us. We were able to secure his financing in just a couple of weeks, building a relationship that has led to multiple referrals and ongoing business.

These relationships feel orchestrated by divine providence rather than human effort. They emerge from conversations we didn't plan, connections we didn't pursue, and introductions we didn't seek. It's as if God is weaving a network of kingdom-minded business relationships that extends far beyond what we could have built through conventional business development.

The Protection That Covers

Not all of our supernatural provision stories are about gaining something; many are about being protected from loss. We've been shielded from industry downturns that devastated competitors. We've avoided regulatory problems that plagued other companies due to our business practices. We've been protected from bad decisions that could have derailed our growth.

During a particularly volatile period in the mortgage industry, when interest rate fluctuations were destroying profit margins for most companies, our pipeline remained remarkably stable. Deals that we thought might fall through continued to close. Interest rate locks happened right on time before rapid market fluctuations. Clients who had postponed doing business suddenly were in the market.

It was as if we were operating under a canopy of divine protection that insulated us from the worst effects of market volatility. While we weren't immune to industry challenges, we consistently experienced better outcomes than our circumstances should have produced.

This protection extends beyond financial metrics to operational challenges as well. We've avoided technology failures that plagued competitors. We've been spared personnel problems that disrupted other companies.

We've navigated regulatory changes more smoothly than firms with far more resources.

The cumulative effect of this protection has been a stability and resilience that exceeds what our size and experience should have provided. We've been able to maintain consistent growth and profitability through market conditions that challenged much larger, more established companies.

These stories of supernatural provision have become more than just company history; they've become testimonies that inspire others to test God's faithfulness in their own businesses and lives. When we share these accounts with other business owners, many are moved to examine their own relationship with money, work, and giving.

Some have started personal tithing for the first time. Others have committed to corporate giving programs. A few have launched their own kingdom-centered businesses. The multiplication effect of our obedience extends far beyond our own company's impact.

But perhaps most importantly, these stories have deepened our own faith and increased our dependence on God. Each example of supernatural provision reminds us that we're not building this business through human strength or wisdom alone. We're partnering with the Creator of the universe, who delights in demonstrating His faithfulness to those who put Him first.

The stories continue to unfold. Each month brings new examples of God's provision, protection, and blessing. We've learned to expect the unexpected, to watch for divine appointments, and to recognize supernatural intervention in the ordinary events of business life.

These testimonies aren't just about us—they're about what God does when His people trust Him completely, when businesses operate by kingdom principles, when faith replaces fear in financial decisions. They're proof that Malachi 3:10 isn't just a historical promise but a present reality for those willing to test God's faithfulness.

"By putting Him first through
our tithing, we've created a
legacy that extends beyond
our bottom line."

11

THE TITHE FOUNDATION—
KINGDOM IMPACT

In 2024, our tithe represented over 62% of company profits. We were humbled and thrilled to return those funds to the Lord to support the local church, Christian education, youth and family services, and ministries serving the homeless.

The Tithe Foundation became the vehicle through which God multiplied our obedience into kingdom impact. We've been able to support pastors, fund Christian schools, assist families in crisis, and contribute to homeless outreach programs. Each dollar given has created ripple effects throughout our community.

The Tithe Foundation wasn't part of our original business plan. When we launched Tithe Lending, we simply committed to giving away 10% of our revenue. But as that giving grew from hundreds to thousands to tens of thousands of dollars, we realized we needed a more strategic approach to maximize kingdom impact.

The foundation was born from a desire to be excellent stewards of the resources God was entrusting to us. Rather than just writing checks to various ministries, we wanted to develop relationships, understand needs, and invest in long-term kingdom building. We wanted our giving to be as intentional and strategic as our business operations.

But the foundation also emerged from a theological conviction: if God was blessing our business because of our tithing commitment, then we had a responsibility to multiply that blessing through wise distribution. We weren't just conduits of giving; we were stewards of multiplication.

The structure of a foundation provided account-ability, transparency, and tax efficiency. But more importantly, it gave us a framework for prayerful deci-sion-making about where God wanted these resources deployed for maximum kingdom impact.

Our approach to giving through the Tithe Foundation reflects the same principles that guide our business oper-ations: excellence, integrity, relationships, and results. We don't just support ministries; we partner with them. We don't just write checks; we build relationships. We don't just give money; we invest in transformation.

Our primary focus areas emerged from prayer, com-munity assessment, and biblical priorities. Supporting the local church became foundational because we believe the church is God's primary vehicle for advancing His kingdom on earth. Christian education received priority because we're investing in the next generation of kingdom leaders. Youth and family services are aligned with our conviction that strong families are essential for healthy communities. Homeless ministries reflected our commitment to serving "the least of these."

Within each focus area, we look for ministries that demonstrate both spiritual vitality and operational excellence. We want to support organizations that share our commitment to biblical truth and practical effectiveness. We invest in ministries that measure both spiritual impact and tangible outcomes.

This strategic approach has allowed us to develop deep partnerships rather than superficial donor relationships. We know the pastors we support, the principals of the schools we fund, and the directors of the programs we sponsor. Our giving has created a network of kingdom relationships that extends our impact far beyond our financial contribution.

One of our largest single areas of investment is support for youth and family services. The foundational impact that we can have in the lives of children in our communities heals a number of wounds and also prevents some of the issues that arise later in adult life. Many of the homeless ministries we have come to love and support are helping to address problems that began as minors. Whether it be assisting services that are working through the foster system, providing a means for daycare and education for teen moms, or elevating high school teens through our leadership programs, we love investing in the next generation where investment may not otherwise exist.

One of our most recent partnerships is with a nonprofit that is transcending the traditional separation of church and state, specifically with foster care youth in need of short-term care. Many single mothers do not have the ability or network to provide short-term (1-2 weeks) oversight for their children in the case of a medical event or another event requiring their attention. When there is no other choice, these children are forced to enter the foster system. Often, they become stuck in the oversight of the state for a year or more.

Keeping children with their biological families is critical. Unfortunately, over 80% of our incarcerated population was once in the state foster system. It gets worse for those on death row. Over 90% come from our state foster systems as a youth. The family is one of the biggest guardrails for our kids when it comes to how they see their worth and value later in life.

The ministry we directly support works with the local church and the state. Families from hundreds of churches volunteer, get vetted and checked, and are made available for short-term care for parents who would otherwise be forced to turn to the state system. They are then reunited with their family when the pressing event or issue has passed.

This is a win/win. The families who volunteer meet the children with the love of Jesus, and provide genuine care. The state is relieved of the workload and responsibility for placement, saving countless hours of time and tens of thousands of dollars in expenses. The biggest winners are the kids themselves. Rather than being placed in a state system, moved from home to home, and potentially being stuck and separated from their parents and siblings, they are loved and then given the opportunity to quickly reunite with their parents and siblings.

At Tithe Foundation, we have been able to assist in expanding these services by funding area director salaries and operational costs to bring ministries to new areas and cities. We want to see youth and families thrive. God wants to see our youth able to experience their full potential. Together, we have been able to help this ministry do its small part in making that happen.

Christian education represents another major focus of our foundation giving. We believe that training children and young adults to think biblically about every area of life is essential for the future of our faith and our culture. Our support has ranged from scholarship assistance for individual students to capital improvements for entire institutions.

One particularly rewarding partnership involved a Christian elementary school that was struggling to expand in one of the neediest areas of our city. The public schools in the area are in the bottom 2% of our state, and the surrounding area has no other alternatives. Just several years ago, nine churches and several other organizations came together to start a Christian school in the area. Students attend at no cost to the family, 100% supported by the vouchers available from the state. Needless to say, the school is forced to run lean. Vouchers provide about ¼ of the funding if these children were to stay with the failing school system around them. The school began with K-2, then expanded to 3rd and 4th grade. Its success drew even more demand from parents and families in the area. The need to expand through the 8th grade quickly became an opportunity and a huge obstacle due to funding concerns. A building was secured for the expansion, but it was in disrepair. It needed everything from plumbing work to basic hygiene upgrades to meet school standards, not counting the desks and supplies required to serve students. As a foundation, we were able to step in and supply help. Our grant moved quickly. From application to funding, we were able to provide a meaningful chunk of necessary funding within weeks.

We've also provided scholarship assistance for families who wanted Christian education for their children but lacked the financial resources. These investments have allowed dozens of students to receive biblically-based education that shapes not just their academic knowledge but also their character, values, and worldview.

Our commitment to serving "the least of these" has also led to significant investment in homeless ministries. This includes supporting homeless shelters, soup kitchens, transitional housing programs, and job training initiatives. But our approach goes beyond meeting immediate needs to addressing root causes and creating pathways to self-sufficiency.

One ministry we support operates a transitional housing and jobs program that provides not just shelter but comprehensive life restoration services. Residents receive housing while participating in addiction recovery programs, job training, financial literacy education, and spiritual discipleship. The program has achieved remarkable success rates in helping people transition from homelessness to stable employment and permanent housing.

Another partnership involves a downtown ministry that provides meals, shower facilities, and clothing assistance while also offering spiritual counseling and practical life skills training. Our funding has allowed them to expand their facilities and hire additional staff, increasing their capacity to serve some of our community's most vulnerable residents.

We've learned that effective homeless ministry requires both compassion and wisdom, both immediate relief and long-term solutions. The ministries we support share our commitment to treating every person with dignity while addressing the complex factors that contribute to homelessness.

The Multiplier Effect

But the foundation represents something deeper than just charitable giving. It's a testament to what happens when we align our business practices with God's principles. By putting Him first through our tithing, we've created a legacy that extends far beyond our company's bottom line.

The most profound realization has been watching how one company's obedience spreads. Other business owners have been inspired to examine their own giving practices. Several dozen businesses have linked with Tithe Foundation to honor God and love others through their work. Others have committed to corporate giving programs. The multiplier effect of faithfulness extends far beyond what we could have imagined.

Our partner businesses and individuals who learned about our foundation approach have signed tithing pledges dedicating their work to the Lord, and committing at least 10% of profits to Kingdom causes. Several entrepreneurs were inspired to launch a business with tithing built into the business model from day one. A real estate agent we work with began donating a portion of her commissions to Christian education after seeing the impact of our school partnerships.

The ripple effects extend to our employees as well. Many team members have increased their personal giving after seeing the foundation's impact. Many have started volunteering with ministries we support. Others have brought their churches into partnership with organizations we fund.

Measuring the true impact of foundation giving requires looking beyond financial metrics to spiritual and social transformation. We track not just how much money we give but how many lives are changed, how many communities are strengthened, how many souls are reached for Christ.

The churches we support have baptized hundreds of new believers. The schools we fund have graduated thousands of students equipped to influence their culture for Christ. The family ministries we sponsor have preserved households, supported pregnant women, and provided hope to struggling families. The homeless programs we support have restored dignity, provided shelter, and transformed lives.

But the ultimate measure of impact may be the multiplication factor. Every dollar we give through the foundation leverages additional giving from others. Every ministry we support becomes stronger and more effective. Every life that's transformed becomes a catalyst for reaching others.

Looking Forward

As Tithe Lending continues to grow, so does the capacity of the Tithe Foundation to impact the kingdom. What started as a simple commitment to give away 10% of our revenue has become a strategic platform for advancing God's work in our community and beyond.

We're constantly seeking new partnerships, evaluating emerging needs, and looking for innovative ways to maximize kingdom impact. We want our giving to be as creative and excellent as our business operations, as strategic and effective as our company leadership.

But we never want to lose sight of the foundation's fundamental purpose: to demonstrate that God blesses businesses that put Him first, to prove that tithing leads to multiplication, to show that kingdom principles work in marketplace realities.

The Tithe Foundation isn't about what we give away—it's about what God does when His people trust Him completely. It's proof that Malachi 3:10 is still true, that divine economics still operate, that faith still moves mountains and multiplies resources.

The foundation represents our attempt to be faithful stewards of the supernatural provision God has given us. But more than that, it represents our invitation to others to test God's faithfulness in their own lives and businesses because the same God who has blessed our obedience is ready to bless theirs.

The impact continues to grow. The kingdom advances. The multiplication expands. And it all started with a simple decision to trust God with 10% of our revenue.

This is what happens when we take God seriously, when we put His kingdom first, when we dare to test His faithfulness. The Tithe Foundation is just the beginning of what God can do through businesses that honor Him. The invitation remains open for others to join this movement of kingdom-centered commerce, faith-based entrepreneurship, and tithing transformation.

PART 3

"The key principle is
consistency and obedience
rather than perfect
precision."

12

STARTING YOUR OWN TEST

Taking the first step in tithing requires both practical mechanics and heart preparation. I'll be honest—those first several tithe checks were interesting to write. I wanted to do it, but still felt a tight grip on allowing those funds to flow back to their source. I was used to deploying them elsewhere, so this took some deliberate practice and reflection.

Before we dive into practical steps, let's acknowledge the internal battle that precedes faithful tithing. For most of us, money represents security, control, and freedom. Writing that first tithe check feels like giving up all three. Your mind will generate every possible reason why this month isn't the right time to start, why your situation is uniquely challenging, and why waiting until you're more financially stable makes sense.

I remember holding my first virtual tithe check for several minutes before hitting send on the offering button. It was the largest amount I'd given at one time to a church. I wanted to do it, but it still went against my prior habits. My practical mind was calculating all the things that money could have purchased, all the bills it could have helped with, all the security it could have provided.

But that's exactly the point. Tithing isn't supposed to feel comfortable—it's supposed to feel like faith. If giving 10% of your income felt easy and natural, it wouldn't be a test of trust. The discomfort you feel is evidence that you're stepping beyond your own ability to control outcomes and into God's realm of provision.

The heart preparation involves recognizing this discomfort as normal and necessary. It means acknowledging that your feelings about money have been shaped by years of cultural conditioning that says accumulation equals security. It requires admitting that you've been operating as if you're the ultimate source of your provision rather than recognizing God as the true provider.

This preparation also involves studying what Scripture says about money, stewardship, and God's character. The more you understand about God's heart for generosity and His track record of faithfulness, the easier it becomes to trust Him with your finances.

The Practical Steps

First, determine your income source and timing. Whether you're salaried, hourly, or self-employed, identify when and how much you receive. The tithe is 10% of your gross income—before taxes, before deductions, before anything else.

This calculation is more straightforward for salaried employees but requires more intentionality for those with variable incomes. If you're in sales, real estate, or consulting, your income may fluctuate significantly from month to month. In these cases, I recommend tithing on each payment as it arrives rather than trying to average your annual income.

For business owners, the calculation involves tithing on the business income that flows to you personally, not necessarily on gross business revenue. However, some business owners choose to tithe on business revenue as well, creating both personal and corporate giving strategies.

The key principle is consistency and obedience rather than perfect precision. God is more interested in your heart posture than your mathematical exactness. Start with a clear understanding of what constitutes your income, then apply the 10% consistently.

Second, choose your destination. Scripture indicates the tithe should go to the "storehouse"—your local church. This isn't about finding the most efficient charity or the cause that tugs at your heartstrings. It's about obedience to God's specific instruction.

The choice of church can be challenging for people who don't have a consistent church home or who have concerns about their church's financial stewardship. However, the principle remains the same: the tithe should support the local body of believers where you receive spiritual nourishment.

If you're between churches or visiting different congregations, choose one where you're receiving consistent spiritual input and commit your tithe there. If you have concerns about financial stewardship, address those through appropriate church channels while continuing to tithe faithfully.

The tithe is distinct from other charitable giving. While supporting parachurch ministries, missionary organizations, and charitable causes is important and biblical, these gifts should be offerings beyond the tithe rather than substitutes for it.

Third, make it automatic if possible. Set up electronic transfers or write the check first, before you pay any other bills. The principle of "first fruits" means God gets the first portion, not what's left over.

Automation removes the monthly decision-making process that can become a source of temptation. When tithing happens automatically, you don't have to wrestle with whether this month is a good time to give or whether other expenses should take priority.

If automatic giving isn't possible through your church, consider writing your tithe check at the beginning of each month and either mailing it or bringing it to the next service. The key is ensuring that the tithe is the first financial priority, not something you hope to get to after other expenses are covered.

For those with irregular income, this might mean tithing immediately when income arrives rather than waiting for month-end calculations. This approach reinforces the first fruits principle and prevents the tithe from being forgotten or rationalized away.

Addressing Common Fears

"What if I can't afford it?" This is the most common concern, and it's exactly why God calls it a test. He wants to prove His faithfulness to provide. Start by tracking your expenses for a month. You might be surprised where money is currently going.

Most people who claim they can't afford to tithe haven't actually examined their spending patterns. We tend to underestimate discretionary expenses while overestimating our fixed costs. A careful review of bank statements often reveals spending on entertainment, dining out, subscriptions, and impulse purchases that exceeds the tithe amount.

The "I can't afford it" fear is really a disguised statement about priorities. What we're actually saying is that we can't afford to tithe while maintaining our current lifestyle. This creates an opportunity to evaluate whether our lifestyle choices align with our stated values.

However, for those facing genuine financial hardship, the principle of faithful giving remains important even if the full 10% isn't immediately possible. God honors movement in the right direction, faithful steps toward obedience, and sacrificial giving, even when the amounts are small.

"What if my church misuses the money?" Your responsibility is obedience, not oversight. Give faithfully and trust God to deal with stewardship issues.

This concern often masks a deeper control issue. We want to ensure that our money is used exactly as we would direct it, which defeats the purpose of giving. When we give our tithe to the church, we're entrusting those resources to the leadership God has placed in authority, trusting Him to guide their decisions and hold them accountable.

If you have serious concerns about financial misman-agement, address those through appropriate church governance channels. Participate in annual meetings, ask questions during budget presentations, and engage in the oversight processes that most churches have in place.

But don't withhold your tithe because of finan-cial concerns. Your obedience to God's command isn't contingent on your church's perfect stewardship. God will handle the accountability issues; your job is faithful giving.

"Should I tithe on gross or net income?" Scripture suggests gross income—the full increase before any deductions.

The biblical principle of "first fruits" implies giving from the full harvest before any portion is set aside for other purposes. Taxes, insurance premiums, and retire-ment contributions are all deductions from your gross income, but they don't represent the actual increase that God has provided.

Tithing on gross income also eliminates the com-plexity of deciding which deductions are legitimate and which aren't. It creates a clear, unambiguous standard that honors the first fruits principle.

For those who find tithing on gross income initially challenging, starting with net income is better than not tithing at all. But the goal should be working toward gross income as your faith and finances allow.

Start where you are. If 10% feels impossible, begin with what you can and work toward the full tithe. God honors faithful steps in the right direction.

The perfect tithe that never gets started is less valuable than the imperfect tithe that begins immediately. If you can only give 2% or 5% initially, start there and commit to increasing that percentage as God provides opportunity.

However, don't use this principle as an excuse to avoid the full tithe indefinitely. Set specific goals and timelines for reaching 10%. Perhaps increase by 1% every three months until you reach the full tithe. The key is having a plan and sticking to it rather than remaining comfortable with partial obedience.

Some people find it helpful to start with a specific dollar amount rather than a percentage, then maintain that amount even as their income fluctuates. This approach can make the initial commitment feel more manageable while building the habit of regular giving.

Pray before you give. Let it be an act of worship, not just a financial transaction.

Tithing should be accompanied by gratitude, recognition of God's provision, and surrender of your financial concerns to His care. Take time to thank God for the income He's provided, acknowledge Him as the source of all your resources, and commit the remaining 90% to His guidance as well.

This prayer doesn't need to be lengthy or formal, but it should be intentional. Use the moment of giving to realign your heart with God's priorities, to remember His faithfulness in the past, and to express trust in His provision for the future.

Some people find it helpful to keep a gratitude journal of God's provision, noting both the income that allows them to tithe and the blessings that follow their faithful giving. This practice reinforces the connection between obedience and blessing.

Remember—this is about heart transformation, not religious duty.

The ultimate goal of tithing isn't compliance with a rule but cultivation of a relationship. God isn't looking for reluctant religious obligation but joyful worship. He wants our hearts, not just our money.

As you begin tithing, pay attention to how it affects your relationship with God, your trust in His provision, and your perspective on money. Notice whether your prayers become more grateful, your giving becomes more joyful, and your financial anxiety begins to decrease.

The heart transformation that accompanies faithful tithing often becomes more valuable than the financial blessings. Learning to trust God with money creates the capacity to trust Him with every area of life.

Overcoming Initial Obstacles

The First Month Challenge: Your first month of tithing will likely be the most difficult. You'll notice the missing money more acutely, question the decision more frequently, and feel the financial adjustment more intensely. This is normal and temporary.

The Emergency Fund Excuse: Many people delay tithing until they've built an adequate emergency fund. While emergency savings are wise, they shouldn't prevent obedience to God's command. Trust that faithful tithing contributes to your long-term financial security rather than detracting from it.

The Debt Payoff Debate: Some financial advisors recommend eliminating all debt before tithing. However, God's command to tithe doesn't include exceptions for debt. In fact, faithful tithing often provides the peace and wisdom needed to address debt more effectively.

The Spousal Disagreement: If you're married and your spouse doesn't support tithing, start with prayer and gentle conversation rather than unilateral action. Look for ways to honor both your spouse and God, perhaps starting with a smaller amount that both of you can agree on.

The Irregular Income Reality: Those with variable incomes often struggle with tithing because they can't predict their monthly ability to give. Consider tithing immediately on each payment received rather than trying to calculate monthly averages.

The First Year Journey

The first year of tithing is typically a journey from reluctance to confidence, from fear to faith, from obligation to opportunity. Most people find that the initial financial adjustment becomes easier within 3-4 months as they learn to live on 90% of their income. After all, it's better to live on 90% God's way than 100% our way.

More importantly, they begin to notice God's faithfulness in unexpected ways—bills that are lower than expected, unexpected income sources, deals that save money, and problems that are resolved without major expense. These experiences build confidence in God's provision and make continuing to tithe feel less risky and more reasonable. Not all of this happens all at once, but those who tithe always have stories of the ways that God makes it work.

By the end of the first year, most faithful tithers report that they can't imagine not tithing. The practice has become integrated into their financial rhythms, their spiritual worship, and their relationship with God. They've learned that obedience leads to blessing, that faith produces peace, and that putting God first doesn't diminish their lives but enriches them.

The test that seemed so frightening at the beginning becomes a source of joy and confidence. The step of faith becomes a lifestyle of trust. The financial sacrifice becomes a spiritual privilege.

"The tithe creates the foundation; offerings build the structure."

13

BEYOND THE TITHE—A LIFE OF GENEROSITY

The tithe is just the beginning of a generous life. Once you establish the foundation of giving God the first 10%, you'll often find your heart expanding toward additional giving opportunities.

The tithe is a requirement—the baseline of obedience. Offerings are gifts beyond the tithe, given as the Spirit leads and as your heart responds to specific needs or opportunities. Both are important, but they serve different purposes.

This distinction is crucial for understanding biblical generosity. The tithe represents our recognition that everything belongs to God and establishes our priorities accordingly. It's not optional, negotiable, or dependent on our feelings about specific causes or circumstances.

Offerings, however, are responsive gifts that flow from a heart aligned with God's through faithful tithing. They represent our partnership with God in addressing specific needs, supporting particular ministries, or responding to His prompting for extraordinary generosity.

The tithe creates the foundation; offerings build the structure. Without the foundation of faithful tithing, our giving tends to be sporadic, emotion-driven, and inconsistent. With the foundation in place, our additional giving becomes more strategic, Spirit-led, and impactful.

Think of the tithe as your baseline commitment to God's kingdom and offerings as your additional investments in specific kingdom opportunities. Both are necessary for a fully biblical approach to money and generosity.

One of the most remarkable effects of faithful tithing is how it changes your perspective on money and possessions. When you regularly give away the first 10% of your income, you begin to see yourself as a steward rather than an owner, as a manager rather than a master of your resources.

This perspective shift creates what I call "loose hands" toward money. You still work hard, plan wisely, and manage carefully, but you hold your resources lightly because you know they ultimately belong to God. This makes additional giving feel natural rather than forced, joyful rather than obligatory.

The heart change also affects how you view opportunities for generosity. Instead of seeing giving as a threat to your security, you begin to see it as an opportunity for partnership with God. Instead of calculating what you'll have left, you start anticipating what God might do through your obedience.

This transformation doesn't happen overnight, but it's one of the most profound benefits of faithful tithing. Your relationship with money changes from anxiety-inducing to worship-enhancing, from security-threatening to kingdom-building.

Spontaneous Giving

As your heart aligns with God's through tithing, you'll become more sensitive to His prompting for additional giving. A single mother needs car repairs. A missionary requiring support. A church building project. These moments become opportunities for offerings beyond the tithe.

The beautiful thing about spontaneous giving is how natural it becomes when your heart is properly aligned through faithful tithing. You begin to notice needs that you might have previously overlooked. You become aware of opportunities for impact that you might have previously ignored.

More importantly, you develop confidence in your ability to give beyond the tithe because you've already proven God's faithfulness in providing for your needs. When you know that God has taken care of you through faithful tithing, you're more willing to trust Him with additional giving.

I remember the first time I felt clearly prompted to give spontaneously beyond our tithe. Since then, we have given this way many times. These experiences have spanned from situations within our extended family where funds were needed, families in our church that were going through significant hardship, and even friends who live in distant states going through a tough set of circumstances. We get to participate in God's moving. We get to partner with him to be a blessing to others, and often bring their hearts closer to Jesus by showing them his love.

These gifts were a turning point in our understanding of offerings. We realized that God doesn't just want our baseline obedience through tithing. He wants to use us as conduits of blessing for specific situations and needs. Our additional giving became a way of participating in His miraculous provision for others.

Planned Generosity

While spontaneous giving responds to immediate needs and Spirit promptings, planned generosity involves strategic thinking about how to maximize kingdom impact through additional giving beyond the tithe.

This might include annual gifts to specific ministries, monthly support for missionaries, quarterly contributions to Christian education, or special offerings for church capital campaigns. Planned generosity allows you to think strategically about causes you want to support consistently, rather than just responding to immediate appeals.

Many families find it helpful to establish an annual giving budget that includes both their tithe and planned offerings. This approach allows them to be intentional about supporting causes they're passionate about while still maintaining flexibility for spontaneous giving opportunities.

The key is ensuring that planned offerings don't become substitutes for the tithe or excuses for avoiding spontaneous generosity. They should enhance your giving strategy rather than complicate it.

Generous living extends beyond money. Your time, skills, and talents are also gifts to be stewarded for God's glory. Volunteer at your church. Mentor

someone in your profession. Use your abilities to serve others without compensation.

The principle of stewardship applies to every resource God has given you, not just your financial resources. Your professional skills, personal experiences, creative abilities, and available time are all gifts that can be deployed for kingdom purposes.

This holistic approach to generosity often becomes more natural after you've established faithful tithing. When you're regularly giving money to God's kingdom, you begin to think about what other resources you could contribute. You start looking for ways to use your non-financial assets for kingdom impact.

For business professionals, this might mean providing pro bono services to nonprofits, mentoring young entrepreneurs, or serving on ministry boards. For skilled tradespeople, it could involve donating labor for church construction projects or home repairs for families in need. For creative individuals, it might mean using artistic abilities to enhance worship services or ministry communications.

The beauty of giving time and talents is that it often provides more personal fulfillment than financial giving alone. When you use your skills to serve others, you experience the joy of seeing your abilities make a direct difference in people's lives.

Throughout the year, various opportunities arise for additional giving beyond your regular tithe and planned offerings. Christmas and Easter often bring special mission offerings. Summer provides opportunities for supporting youth camps and mission trips. Fall typically includes education-related giving opportunities.

Rather than viewing these seasonal appeals as burdens or interruptions to your financial planning, approach them as opportunities for additional kingdom investment. Pray about each opportunity, consider how it aligns with your values and God's prompting, and respond with the same faithfulness that characterizes your tithing.

Some families establish a separate "special offerings" fund that they contribute to monthly, building resources for these seasonal opportunities. This approach allows them to respond generously to special appeals without disrupting their regular budget or compromising their tithing commitment.

Teaching the Next Generation

One of the greatest impacts of faithful tithing is how it shapes your children's understanding of money and generosity. They watch you write those checks, see your priorities in action, and learn that

God comes first. This creates a legacy of generosity that can span generations.

Children are remarkably observant about their parents' relationship with money. They notice whether you argue about finances, whether you're generous with others, and whether you give cheerfully or grudgingly. Your approach to tithing and offering becomes a powerful teaching tool that shapes their understanding of money, stewardship, and priorities.

Make your giving visible and intentional in your family discussions. Let your children see you writing the checks so they understand that God comes first. Explain why you're supporting specific ministries. Involve them in age-appropriate decisions about family giving. This transparency helps them understand that generosity is a natural part of following God rather than an unusual burden.

Raise your children to understand that everything belongs to God, that we're stewards rather than owners, and that giving isn't about what we can afford—it's about trusting the One who provides everything.

This stewardship mindset is one of the most valuable gifts you can give your children. In a culture that promotes materialism and consumerism, teaching your children that they're managers rather than owners of their resources provides a foundation for lifelong contentment and generosity.

Start early with age-appropriate lessons. Help young children divide their allowance into giving, saving, and spending categories. Encourage teenagers to tithe from their job income. Involve adult children in family giving decisions and ministry support choices.

The goal is to raise children who see generous giving as normal and natural rather than exceptional and sacrificial. When generosity is modeled consistently at home, it becomes an integral part of their character rather than an external religious obligation.

As your understanding of stewardship matures, you may begin thinking about how to structure your estate and long-term assets for continued kingdom impact after your death. This might involve charitable trusts, ministry bequests, or family foundations that perpetuate your giving values across generations.

Legacy giving allows you to multiply the impact of your lifetime generosity by ensuring that your resources continue supporting kingdom causes even after you're gone. It also provides opportunities to involve your children and grandchildren in ongoing giving decisions, teaching them stewardship principles through practical experience.

While legacy giving involves complex legal and financial considerations that require professional guidance, the basic principle is simple: view your accumulated assets as kingdom resources to be deployed strategically for maximum eternal impact.

The Joy of Partnership

Perhaps the most surprising discovery for many faithful givers is how much joy comes from partnering with God in His work through generous giving. What begins as obedience to the tithe command often evolves into eager anticipation of opportunities to give beyond the tithe.

This joy comes from seeing your resources make a tangible difference in advancing God's kingdom, supporting His people, and meeting genuine needs. It comes from knowing that your giving is creating an eternal impact that will outlast your earthly life.

But the deepest joy comes from the intimate partnership with God that generous giving creates. When you're regularly looking for ways to give beyond the tithe, you're constantly asking God where He wants to deploy resources, how He wants to use your stewardship, and what kingdom opportunities He wants you to support.

This ongoing conversation about giving deepens your relationship with God and increases your sensitivity to His voice. Generous living becomes a form of ongoing worship that keeps your heart aligned with His priorities and your resources available for His purposes.

The tithe establishes the foundation, but a life of generosity builds the legacy. Both are necessary for experiencing the full joy and impact that God intends for our stewardship of His resources.

"The beautiful thing about this vision is its multiplication factor."

14

THE $161 BILLION VISION

The potential impact of faithful Christian tithing in America is staggering. If American Christians simply obeyed this basic biblical principle, we would release $161 billion annually for kingdom purposes. Let me break down what this could accomplish:

To understand the magnitude of this opportunity, we need to grasp the current state of Christian giving in America. According to recent research, there are approximately 205 million Christians in the United States. The median household income for Christian families is roughly $52,000 annually. If every Christian household tithed 10% of their income, we would see an immediate and dramatic increase in kingdom resources.

Currently, Christians give an average of 2.5% of their income to religious and charitable causes. This means we're operating at one-quarter of our biblical potential. The $161 billion figure represents what becomes available when we move from 2.5% to 10%—when we transition from cultural Christianity to biblical obedience.

But this isn't just about percentages and statistics. This is about the difference between the kingdom of God operating on fumes versus operating at full capacity. This is about the church fulfilling its mandate to serve the world versus struggling to keep its doors open. This is about individual believers experiencing God's faithfulness versus living in financial anxiety.

The $161 billion isn't theoretical money—it's real income that's currently being directed toward earthly accumulation instead of eternal investment. Every dollar represents a choice between temporary pleasure and permanent impact, between personal security and kingdom advancement, between earthly treasure and heavenly reward.

Educational Transformation

With $12 million per school (construction plus first-year operating costs), we could open 13,416 Christian schools annually. Imagine the impact on our children, our culture, and our future when Christian education becomes accessible everywhere.

The educational crisis in America isn't just about academic performance—it's about worldview formation. Public education, by constitutional design, cannot include biblical truth in its curriculum. Private secular education often promotes values that contradict

Christian beliefs. Christian families are left with limited options for educating their children in environments that reinforce rather than undermine their faith.

$161 billion could change this reality completely. Instead of Christian education being accessible only to wealthy families, it could become available in every community across America. Instead of Christian parents having to choose between financial strain and spiritual compromise, they could access an excellent education that aligns with their values.

Each $12 million investment would create more than just a school—it would create a community trans-formation center. Christian schools become hubs for family strengthening, community outreach, and cultural influence. They graduate students who understand their purpose in God's kingdom, their responsibility to serve others, and their calling to influence society for Christ.

The ripple effects extend beyond individual families to entire communities. Areas with strong Christian schools often see decreased crime rates, increased community cohesion, and enhanced economic development. The schools become magnets for Christian families, creating concentrations of kingdom-minded citizens who influ-ence local politics, business practices, and cultural norms.

But perhaps most importantly, these schools would train the next generation of Christian leaders—pastors, missionaries, business executives, politicians, teachers, doctors, and entrepreneurs who understand that their vocations are callings to serve God's kingdom. The long-term cultural impact of 13,000+ new Christian schools annually would be incalculable.

Ending Hunger

At $2.50 per meal, including logistics, $161 billion could serve 64.4 billion meals per year. We could literally end hunger in America and make a massive dent in world hunger simultaneously.

Hunger isn't just a global problem—it's a crisis in our own communities. According to Feeding America, 38 million Americans, including 12 million children, experience food insecurity. Meanwhile, 828 million people worldwide don't have enough food to live active, healthy lives.

The $2.50 per meal calculation includes not just food costs but the entire infrastructure needed to identify hungry people, prepare nutritious meals, and deliver them consistently. This comprehensive approach would create sustainable feeding programs rather than sporadic charitable efforts.

In America, 64.4 billion meals annually would mean every food-insecure person could receive three nutritious meals every day for an entire year, with meals left over for emergency situations and community outreach. We could eliminate childhood hunger, senior citizen malnutrition, and homelessness-related starvation.

Globally, this level of meal provision would address hunger in the world's most impoverished regions. We could fund feeding programs in refugee camps, drought-stricken areas, war-torn regions, and economically collapsed nations. These programs wouldn't just provide temporary relief but would create infrastructure for long-term food security.

The spiritual impact would be equally significant. Every meal becomes an opportunity to share the Gospel, to demonstrate Christ's love in practical ways, and to build relationships that open doors for evangelism. Feeding programs become platforms for church planting, discipleship, and community transformation.

Youth Impact

With 49,538 youth centers opened annually at $3.25 million each, every community could have safe, Christ-centered places for children and teenagers. The impact on crime, education, and spiritual development would be immeasurable.

The youth crisis in America is reaching epidemic proportions. Teen suicide rates are climbing. Drug and alcohol abuse among adolescents is increasing. Academic performance is declining. Mental health issues are proliferating. Many communities lack safe spaces where young people can gather, learn, and develop healthy relationships.

Christian youth centers address multiple needs simultaneously. They provide safe spaces for recreation and socialization. They offer tutoring and academic support. They create mentorship opportunities with caring adults. They present the Gospel in age-appropriate ways. They teach life skills and character development.

Each $3.25 million investment would create a comprehensive youth facility with recreational equipment, educational resources, meeting spaces, and programming budgets. These centers would serve hundreds of young people annually, creating positive alternatives to destructive activities.

The crime prevention impact alone would justify the investment. Communities with quality youth programs consistently show reduced juvenile crime rates, decreased gang involvement, and improved school performance. But the spiritual impact extends far beyond crime prevention to life transformation and eternal salvation.

These centers would become recruitment grounds for future missionaries, pastors, Christian business leaders, and kingdom-minded citizens. They would interrupt generational cycles of poverty, addiction, and hopelessness by providing young people with purpose, direction, and spiritual foundation.

Global Evangelism

Funding 53.67 million mission trips at $3,000 per person would accelerate the spread of the Gospel worldwide. We could reach unreached people groups, support indigenous churches, and fulfill the Great Commission in our generation.

The Great Commission to "make disciples of all nations" remains unfulfilled more than 2,000 years after Jesus spoke these words. Despite centuries of missionary effort, approximately 3 billion people still have minimal access to the Gospel. Hundreds of people groups remain completely unreached.

53.67 million mission trips annually would represent the largest evangelistic mobilization in human history. This wouldn't just be short-term mission trips but a comprehensive approach including career missionaries, church planting teams, Bible translators, medical missionaries, and indigenous church support.

The $3,000 per person calculation covers transportation, training, support materials, and in-country ministry expenses. This level of funding would make mission participation accessible to believers from every economic background, not just those who can afford international travel.

The multiplication effect would be extraordinary. Each missionary trip creates ongoing relationships between sending churches and receiving communities. Short-term mission participants often become long-term supporters of international ministry. Local believers are encouraged and equipped to continue evangelistic work.

But perhaps most importantly, this level of mission activity would fulfill biblical prophecy about the Gospel being preached to every nation before Christ's return. We could literally see the completion of the Great Commission in our generation through faithful tithing.

Clean Water Access

Building 16.1 million wells at $10,000 each would provide clean water access globally. Each well serves 500-1,000 people, meaning we could solve the world's clean water crisis in a single year of faithful tithing.

Access to clean water is one of the most basic human needs, yet 2 billion people worldwide lack safely managed drinking water at home. Water-related diseases kill more children than AIDS, malaria, and measles combined. Women and children often spend hours daily collecting water instead of attending school or generating income.

The $10,000 per well calculation includes drilling, pump installation, maintenance training, and community education. This comprehensive approach ensures long-term sustainability rather than temporary solutions.

16.1 million wells serving an average of 750 people each would provide clean water access to over 12 billion people—more than the current global population. This means we could not only solve the current clean water crisis but also create infrastructure for future population growth.

The health impacts would be immediate and dramatic. Waterborne diseases would plummet. Child mortality rates would decrease. Productivity would increase as people spend less time collecting water and more time on education and economic activities.

The spiritual opportunities would be equally significant. Wells become gathering places for communities. Drilling teams can share the Gospel while providing this essential service. Local churches can use wells as platforms for outreach and discipleship.

Clean water often opens hearts to the Gospel in ways that words alone cannot. When people experience practical love through clean water access, they become receptive to the spiritual truth about living water that Jesus provides.

Bible Translation

With $550,000 per language for translation and printing, we could fund Bible translations for all remaining 3,000 languages needing God's Word. Every people group could have Scripture in their native tongue.

Despite centuries of translation work, approximately 3,000 languages still lack complete Bible translations. Many people groups have no Scripture in their native language, forcing them to learn a second language to access God's Word. This creates barriers to evangelism, discipleship, and church development.

The $550,000 per language calculation includes linguist training, translation work, community checking, printing, and distribution. This comprehensive approach ensures accurate, culturally appropriate translations that serve communities for generations.

Funding translation for all remaining languages would represent the completion of one of Christianity's most important tasks—making God's Word accessible to every people group on earth. This would fulfill biblical mandates to take the Gospel to every nation and provide Scripture for discipleship and church growth.

The cultural impact extends beyond evangelism to education and development. Bible translation often involves creating written forms of oral languages, developing literacy programs, and preserving cultural heritage. Translation projects frequently become catalysts for community development and social progress.

Bible translation is often the foundation for effective church planting and discipleship. When people can read God's Word in their heart language, they can develop indigenous church leadership, create culturally appropriate worship, and share the Gospel effectively within their communities.

The Multiplication Factor

This isn't just about funding ministry—it's about serving billions and transforming generations in Jesus' name. Your individual tithe isn't just a personal act of obedience; it's participation in the greatest wealth transfer in history for kingdom purposes.

The beautiful thing about this vision is its multiplication factor. Every school trains teachers who start more schools. Every meal program creates volunteers who start more feeding ministries. Every youth center raises leaders who plant more churches. Every well dug opens communities that welcome more missionaries. Every Bible translated enables indigenous evangelists who reach more people groups.

The $161 billion represents first-year funding, but the long-term impact multiplies exponentially. Schools educate students who become Christian leaders. Feeding programs create healthy communities that contribute to society. Youth centers raise up missionaries and pastors. Wells enable communities to thrive and become self-sustaining. Bible translations create indigenous churches that spread the Gospel without ongoing external support.

This vision isn't dependent on government programs, secular philanthropy, or corporate social responsibility initiatives. It's entirely achievable through the obedience of ordinary Christians to a basic biblical command. It doesn't require new laws, technological breakthroughs, or international agreements. It simply requires believers to do what God has always asked them to do—give Him the first tenth of their income.

Your individual tithe may seem small compared to a $161 billion vision, but it's an essential component. Every school, every meal, every youth center, every mission trip, every well, every Bible translation depends on faithful believers like you choosing obedience over accumulation, kingdom priorities over personal preferences.

The question isn't whether this vision is achievable—it absolutely is. The question is whether American Christians will choose to make it a reality through faithful tithing. The resources exist. The infrastructure is available.

The need is documented. The only missing component is widespread obedience to God's clear command.

This is what becomes possible when God's people take His Word seriously, when individual believers trust His promises, when churches teach biblical stewardship, and when families prioritize kingdom investment over earthly accumulation. The $161 billion vision isn't just a dream—it's a calling to every Christian who wants to participate in the greatest kingdom advancement opportunity in history.

"I've discovered that tithing isn't a destination; it's a journey."

15

THE TEST THAT NEVER ENDS

God's use of tithing to shape hearts continues throughout our lives. As I've grown in faith and business, I've discovered that 10% was just the beginning. God sometimes asks for more as our capacity and trust increase.

When I first started tithing, I thought of it as a destination—a spiritual milestone to achieve and then maintain. I imagined that once I consistently gave 10% of my income to God, I would have passed the test and could move on to other areas of spiritual growth.

But I've discovered that tithing isn't a destination; it's a journey. It's not a test you pass once; it's a discipline that continues to shape your heart, refine your character, and deepen your relationship with God throughout your entire life.

Ongoing Refinement: Each month's tithe continues to refine my heart, reminding me of priorities and dependencies. The discipline never becomes automatic in the sense of being thoughtless—it remains a conscious act of worship and trust.

This ongoing refinement is one of tithing's greatest benefits. Just when you think you've mastered trust in God's provision, circumstances arise that test your faith at new levels. Your income increases, and suddenly 10% feels like a larger amount than before. Unexpected expenses emerge, and the tithe becomes more challenging to prioritize. Economic uncertainty creates anxiety about giving when you feel like you should be hoarding.

Each of these situations becomes an opportunity for deeper trust, greater faith, and stronger dependency on God. The tithe that felt routine last month becomes a fresh test of your priorities this month. The discipline that seemed established gets challenged by new circumstances that require renewed surrender.

I've found that God uses the regular rhythm of tithing to keep my heart aligned with His. When I start becoming attached to money or possessions, the monthly tithe reminds me that everything belongs to Him. When I begin trusting in my own ability to provide, the act of giving away the first tenth realigns my dependence on His provision.

The refinement isn't just about money—it's about character. Tithing teaches patience when the check is due, but income is delayed. It builds faith when expenses are high, but the tithe remains the same. It develops generosity when opportunities for additional giving arise. It cultivates contentment when the remaining 90% must cover all other needs.

As God proves faithful in honoring your tithe, your capacity for trust and generosity often expands. What felt like a huge step of faith initially becomes a comfortable routine, creating space for God to invite you into greater levels of giving and kingdom investment.

This expansion doesn't always mean giving more money—sometimes it means giving differently. Perhaps God calls you to support specific ministries, individuals, or causes beyond your regular tithe. Maybe he invites you to fund mission trips, sponsor children, or contribute to building projects.

The expansion might involve time and talents rather than just finances. Faithful tithers often find themselves more willing to volunteer, serve, and use their professional skills for kingdom purposes. The heart change that comes from regular giving creates openness to other forms of sacrifice and service.

For business owners, expanding capacity might mean implementing kingdom principles throughout their operations—not just personal tithing but corporate giving, ethical business practices, employee care, and community service. The faithfulness you develop through personal tithing often translates into broader kingdom-minded thinking about all your resources and responsibilities.

Business Applications

Tithe Lending's commitment to corporate tithing has shown me that these principles work at organizational levels, too. When businesses operate on kingdom principles, employees find purpose, customers receive better service, and the entire culture transforms.

The transition from personal tithing to corporate tithing represented a new level of faith testing. Giving away 10% of personal income is one thing; giving away 10% of business revenue before paying salaries, rent, or operating expenses requires an entirely different level of trust.

But the principles that work in personal finances translate remarkably well to business operations. When a company commits to putting God first through corporate tithing, it creates a culture that attracts employees who want their work to have meaning beyond just generating profits.

Our team members regularly comment on the different atmosphere at Tithe Lending compared to their previous workplaces. They know that their efforts are contributing to kingdom advancement through our corporate tithe. They see their daily work as a ministry rather than just employment. They experience purpose that transcends transaction processing and client service.

This sense of purpose translates into better customer service, higher employee retention, and increased productivity. When people understand that their work contributes to feeding hungry children, supporting pastors, and funding Christian education, they approach their tasks with greater care and commitment.

The corporate tithing also creates accountability that enhances business practices. When you know that your business methods and client relationships reflect on the kingdom causes you support, you're motivated to operate with exceptional integrity and excellence.

Increasing Faith: As God proves faithful with the 10%, He sometimes invites us into greater generosity. Special offerings, additional kingdom investments, and expanded giving become natural expressions of growing trust.

This increasing faith doesn't develop overnight, but it's one of the most rewarding aspects of faithful tithing. Each time God provides for your needs despite your giving, your confidence in His faithfulness grows. Each blessing that follows obedience increases your willingness to trust Him with greater levels of generosity.

The progression often looks like this: faithful tithing leads to recognition of God's provision, which leads to gratitude, which leads to desire for additional giving, which leads to special offerings, which leads to even greater provision, which leads to expanding generosity. It's a virtuous cycle that deepens your relationship with God while increasing your kingdom impact.

But the increasing faith isn't just about giving more money—it's about trusting God with larger decisions, greater risks, and more significant life changes. The person who learns to trust God with 10% of their income often becomes willing to trust Him with career changes, ministry opportunities, and life transitions that require even greater faith.

Generational Impact

One of the most profound aspects of the test that never ends is its impact on future generations. Children who grow up in homes where tithing is practiced consistently develop entirely different perspectives on money, stewardship, and trust in God.

These children learn that financial security comes from God's faithfulness rather than human accumulation. They observe parents making decisions based on biblical principles rather than cultural norms. They witness God's provision in response to faithful giving, creating foundations for their own future trust in His character.

But the generational impact extends beyond individual families to entire communities. Churches with strong tithing cultures create environments where children learn generosity as normal Christian behavior. Communities with high levels of Christian giving become known for their care for the poor, support for education, and concern for spiritual needs.

The test that never ends becomes a legacy that shapes not just your own spiritual development but the spiritual formation of everyone around you. Your faithful tithing becomes a testimony that influences others to trust God with their resources, creating multiplication that extends far beyond your individual obedience.

Eternal Perspective

The ultimate goal isn't just financial obedience— it's laying up treasures in heaven rather than accumulating earthly wealth. My former vision of retirement involved relaxing, golfing, and enjoying accumulated possessions. Now I understand that alignment with God's heart leads to purposes that transcend traditional retirement.

This shift in perspective represents one of the most significant changes that faithful tithing produces. When you regularly invest 10% of your income in God's kingdom, you begin to think about all your resources differently. You start evaluating decisions based on eternal impact rather than just temporal benefit.

The traditional American dream of accumulating enough wealth to stop working and focus on personal pleasure begins to feel empty and purposeless. Instead, you find yourself drawn to a vision of continued service, ongoing contribution, and eternal investment that extends throughout your entire life.

This doesn't mean working until you die or never enjoying rest and recreation. It means finding your primary satisfaction in kingdom advancement rather than personal accumulation, in eternal investment rather than earthly accumulation, in spiritual legacy rather than material inheritance.

We're called to continued service and investment in His kingdom. This isn't about working forever, but about understanding that our hearts find satisfaction in eternal investment rather than temporal accumulation.

The hearts that have been shaped by faithful tithing often find traditional retirement unsatisfying. The purpose and meaning that come from kingdom investment create an appetite for continued contribution that transcends conventional ideas about life stages and career phases.

This might mean transitioning to ministry roles, volunteer service, or kingdom-centered businesses that prioritize impact over income. It could involve mentoring, teaching, or consulting that uses professional skills for kingdom purposes. It often includes increased giving as accumulated resources become available for larger kingdom investments.

The goal isn't activity for its own sake but alignment with God's heart that finds fulfillment in eternal purposes rather than temporal pleasures. The test that never ends becomes a lifestyle of kingdom-focused living that continues until we transition from earth to heaven.

The Joy of the Journey

Perhaps the most surprising discovery for many faithful tithers is how much joy the ongoing test provides. What begins as difficult obedience often evolves into eager anticipation of opportunities to give. The discipline that initially required great faith becomes a source of spiritual confidence and satisfaction.

This joy comes from multiple sources: the pleasure of partnership with God in His work, the satisfaction of seeing your resources make eternal difference, the peace that comes from proper priorities, and the confidence that develops from experiencing God's faithfulness repeatedly.

But the deepest joy comes from the relationship with God that faithful tithing cultivates. The monthly discipline becomes a regular conversation with your heavenly Father about His work, His priorities, and His purposes. The ongoing test becomes an opportunity for deepening intimacy with the One who provides everything you need and uses everything you give.

The test that never ends isn't a burden—it's a privilege. It's an ongoing invitation to participate in the greatest kingdom advancement opportunity in history. It's a lifelong journey of growing trust, expanding generosity, and increasing impact that continues until we see Jesus face to face.

Every month brings new opportunities to pass the test, to trust God's faithfulness, to participate in His work, and to experience the joy of kingdom partnership. The test that never ends becomes the foundation for a life of purpose, meaning, and eternal significance that transcends anything earthly accumulation could provide.

"The heart behind God's call
to tithe is about our hearts
becoming more like His."

CONCLUSION

PASS THE TEST

Two paths stretch before every reader of this book. One leads to continued self-reliance, where we manage our own resources according to our own wisdom, maintaining control but missing the adventure of partnership with God. The other leads to stepping into God's abundance through the simple act of faithful tithing.

I've walked both paths. I can testify that the path of self-reliance, no matter how successful it appears, leads to emptiness. The path of faithful giving, even when it looks risky, leads to purpose, peace, and supernatural provision.

We live in a generation that has forgotten how to trust God with finances. Despite being the wealthiest nation in Earth's history, our giving has declined. But this creates an incredible opportunity. We could be part of the greatest wealth transfer in history—not from one generation to another, but from earthly accumulation to eternal investment.

The choice isn't just personal—it's cultural. It's generational. It's eternal.

When you choose to tithe, you're not just changing your own financial future; you're joining a movement that could transform America, reshape Christianity, and accelerate the advancement of God's kingdom worldwide. You're stepping into a legacy that extends far beyond your individual life into the lives of countless others who will be touched by kingdom resources deployed through faithful stewardship.

A Personal Challenge

When I think about where my heart was prior to tithing, I honestly cannot land on a firm place. Since embracing the tithe, my heart has been firmly planted near the foot of the cross, tied far more closely to Christ. I've embraced Him in my life, how He wants to work, and I am far more comfortable with my treasure being with and near Him.

If I had to answer the question—where was my treasure before, and therefore my heart—I can see clearly now. I had heavy investments in real estate. My heart was trapped inside my home. I had my eye on my investment properties constantly, looked at short-term booking revenues, tracked appreciation values, and was wrapped up in how I could leverage their equity to acquire more.

I didn't love these properties—I loved money, and the leverage these homes provided enabled me to access more of it. Jesus' warning about serving two masters proved true: "No one can serve two masters. Either you will hate the one and love the other, or you will be devoted to one and despise the other. You cannot serve both God and money" (Matthew 6:24).

My devotion was to gaining more earthly wealth. Looking back, I cannot recall having an end in mind. There wasn't a magic number of properties or net worth that would have put an end to the madness. More was the goal. More meant more security, more insulation from future downturns, more evidence that I was winning the race against time.

What a terrible plan I had. Pedal to the metal, full action force at all times to accumulate as much as possible, with the goal of someday applying the brake pedal and stopping. Now that I see it from a bird's eye view, that entire thing looks less like a fairy tale ending in retirement, but a bad dream of exhaustion ending in a meaningless existence of nothingness.

The Heart Transformation

But here's what I discovered: God's heart deeply wants nothing more than for me to invest in the gifts and purpose that I've been given from the divine. His heart leaps when mine aligns with his. When we are in sync together, serving together, sharing and spreading his love with humanity, while attracting those who don't yet know him to his son Jesus. This sounds like so much fun. Far more meaningful than retreating privately into a manufactured world of comforts.

The answer I stumbled on wasn't specifically for me. It was specifically for HIM! By aligning my heart with God's, I magnify his glory through HIS creation. He is glorified. And when that happens, his light can shine brighter through me. My purpose grows. What an incredible feedback loop. I align with Christ, God is glorified, others are served, my light shines brighter, my heart grows in love, my mission and meaning are solidified, my time on earth impacts eternity, and I store more treasure in heaven.

No, what was the guardrail that began to transform my former thinking into this newfound revelation? You guessed it. The tithe.

This transformation isn't unique to my experience. It's available to every believer who takes the step of faith that tithing requires. The same heart change that redirected my life from meaningless accumulation to purposeful service is waiting for you. The same peace that replaced my financial anxiety is available through your obedience. The same joy that comes from partnership with God can become your daily reality.

The heart behind God's call to tithe is about our hearts becoming more like His. With every step of trust and obedience, we draw closer to Him. Tithing helps us grow in love for God as we begin to truly know Him. Not just as our provider, but as the source of all things.

Before examining the ways our heart works, we must clearly understand the heart of God. If our goal is to align and become more and more like Jesus each day, we should examine what tithing is further bringing us into alignment. Luckily, God doesn't make us guess. He shows us in his word what His heart looks like.

Ezekiel 36:25-28 reveals God's transformational heart:

"I will sprinkle clean water on you, and you will be clean; I will cleanse you from all your impurities and from all your idols. I will give you a new heart and put a new spirit in you; I will remove from you your heart of stone and give you a heart of flesh. And I will put my Spirit in you and move you to follow my decrees and be careful to keep my laws. Then you will live in the land

I gave your ancestors; you will be my people, and I will be your God."

Here we see God's heart's desire to transform us. He loves us and calls us back to him not out of fear or judgment, but out of pure love for us. His desire is to cleanse us. He wants us to live in the ways that he has called us to, and wants nothing more than for us to have a heart that houses his spirit.

I've seen this take place in those who have fully understood the tithe. Men and women who are a part of our Tithe Foundation efforts are tithing consistently out of their businesses. I almost never hear a word spoken about the financial aspect of these actions. What do I hear? I hear countless stories of the ways they see God show up inside the walls of their business. The halls and the walls where their employees work have been cleansed in a way. The spirit that moves through the conversations with clients and the typed words of emails can be felt by those aware of what's happened in the heart of the company they represent.

Luke 15:20 shows us God's heart when we return to Him:

"So he got up and went to his father. But while he was still a long way off, his father saw him and was filled with compassion for him; he ran to his son, threw his arms around him, and kissed him."

This passage from the story of the Prodigal Son reveals the heart of God overjoyed at a pivot back toward him. A son who was lost and had gone his own way returns. God's heart leaps when we return to the path that he's called us to.

As I've consulted and learned more about men and women who desire to follow God, but are ashamed of their past performances, I see this parable resurface often. For many, beginning to tithe and put God first from this provision perspective sheds light on the ways they have viewed money and resources in the past. The truth about money is that for most Americans, it has indeed become an idol.

Beginning to tithe brings our past views of money and our past activities pursuing it into the light. Like the prodigal son, many of us feel unworthy of the compassion given to us by God in this area. We must remember that God knows every detail of every step we've taken in every area of our lives. Including the ways we've handled the resources he's provided. His call is to move back down the path toward him. So just start.

Proverbs 4:23 gives us crucial guidance: "Above all else, guard your heart, for everything you do flows from it."

This verse doesn't say "Make sure to pay attention to your heart every now and then." It says "ABOVE ALL ELSE." God is after our hearts. More than any other thing, because everything we do flows from it. EVERYTHING. Our heart is the literal source of all things in our lives.

Just as our physical heart requires protection and healthy habits to function properly, our spiritual heart needs the same care. The tithe functions as a spiritual exercise for our heart—a regular discipline that keeps our relationship with money and God healthy and aligned.

Where my treasure is, my heart will be, and more than likely so will my attention and energy. When we tithe regularly, our heart begins to grow closer and closer to our local church community. The fruit of our lives becomes easier to see as it ripens and is consumed by others in need. It gets contagious.

The tithe is like a spiritual prescription to turn the flow of our hearts back up to full capacity. When we have physical heart issues, we are typically prescribed medications, new diets, exercise, and sometimes, in extreme cases, an invasive surgery to do major repair. But the good news is that as long as we're still alive, we have time to course correct for our future.

The Promise Renewed

God's faithfulness to those who trust Him hasn't changed. Malachi 3:10 still stands: "Test me in this... and see if I will not throw open the floodgates of heaven and pour out so much blessing that there will not be room enough to store it."

I've tested Him. I've found Him faithful. Not just in business success, but in peace that passes understanding, purpose that transcends circumstances, and joy that comes from partnership with the Creator of the universe.

This promise isn't just for me—it's for you. It's for every believer who has the courage to take God at His word, to trust His character, and to step into the adventure of faithful giving. The same God who has provided for me wants to demonstrate His faithfulness to you.

The promise comes with a guarantee: God cannot lie. His character is unchanging. His word is eternal. What he promises, He delivers. When He invites you to test Him, He's not worried about the outcome—He's confident in His ability to prove His faithfulness.

The Vision Realized

Imagine a church that tithes faithfully. Imagine American Christians releasing $161 billion annually for kingdom purposes. Imagine the transformation—not just in our communities and world, but in our own hearts as we learn to trust the God who provides everything.

This isn't just a dream. It's a mathematical certainty if God's people simply obey His clear command. The resources exist. The infrastructure is in place. The needs are documented. The only missing component is obedience.

But this vision starts with individual believers like you making individual decisions to trust God with their finances. It begins with single families choosing to test God's faithfulness through tithing. It grows through one person at a time, discovering that God's way is better than their way.

You have the opportunity to be part of the greatest kingdom advancement initiative in history, not through some complex strategy or innovative program, but through simple obedience to a biblical command that has existed for thousands of years.

Your Moment of Decision

This isn't just a dream. It's an invitation. The test is before you. The choice is yours.

Will you test God in this? Will you join the adventure of faithful giving? Will you discover what He can do when you put Him first?

Right now, as you finish reading this book, you stand at the same crossroads I faced years ago. You can close this book and continue managing your finances the same way you always have, trusting in your own wisdom and maintaining control over your resources.

Or you can take the step of faith that transforms everything—the decision to honor God with the first tenth of your income and trust Him to provide for your needs.

The decision you make in the next few days will determine not just your financial future, but your spiritual trajectory. It will affect not just your bank account, but your relationship with God. It will impact not just your family's security, but your legacy for generations to come.

The tithe changed my life. It can change yours ,too. It's time to return to this principle in America and allow it to transform not just our individual hearts, but our entire culture.

You don't need to wait until you feel ready. You don't need to wait until your income increases. You don't need to wait until your circumstances improve. You need to start where you are, with what you have, trusting that God will meet you in your obedience.

The first tithe check you write will be the hardest. The second will be easier. By the end of your first year, you'll wonder how you ever lived without the peace, purpose, and provision that faithful tithing provides.

But you have to start. You have to take the first step. You have to make the decision that faith requires—to trust God's word more than your own understanding, to believe His promises more than your fears, to act on His commands despite your circumstances.

Pass the Test

Pass the test.

Trust the Provider.

Join the transformation.

God is waiting to show you what He can do.

The test isn't about your ability to afford tithing—it's about your willingness to trust God's ability to provide. It's not about your financial circumstances—it's about your spiritual condition. It's not about the money you give—it's about the heart that gives it.

God has been waiting for this moment—the moment when you decide to trust Him completely with your finances. He's been preparing blessings to pour out on your obedience. He's been orchestrating circumstances to demonstrate His faithfulness to your stewardship.

All that remains is your decision.

Will you pass the test?

The adventure of a lifetime awaits your answer. The transformation you've been longing for is one tithe check away. The peace you've been seeking is found in surrender to the God who provides everything.

Test Him. Trust Him. Tithe faithfully.

And watch what the God of the universe does when you put Him first.

Your story of supernatural provision is about to begin. Your testimony of God's faithfulness is waiting to be written. Your legacy of generous stewardship is ready to unfold.

The test is before you.

The choice is yours.

The time is now.

Pass the test.